Mazo de la Roche, 1879-1961.

Illustration: Magali Lefrançois.

Mazo de la Roche

Heather Kirk

Heather Kirk is a writer and teacher living in Barrie, Ontario. Her writing has been published in many periodicals, including *Books in Canada, Canadian Children's Literature, Canadian Literature, Canadian Woman Studies, Contemporary Verse II, Literary Review of Canada, Quill & Quire*, and *Wascana Review*. Her work has also been broadcast on radio.

Heather Kirk has published two teen novels, *Warsaw Spring* (2001) and *A Drop of Rain* (2004), and a rewrite of the classic Canadian novel, *Wacousta* (2005).

She holds a B.A. from Dalhousie University, an M.A. from the University of Toronto, and an M.A. from York University, where she specialized in Canadian literature. She has taught English at the University of Alberta, the University of Warsaw, Grande Prairie Regional College, and Georgian College.

For more information, visit Heather Kirk's website: http://www.heatherkirk.ca.

In the same collection

Ven Begamudré, *Isaac Brock: Larger Than Life*.
Lynne Bowen, *Robert Dunsmuir: Laird of the Mines*.
Kate Braid, *Emily Carr: Rebel Artist*.
Kathryn Bridge, *Phyllis Munday: Mountaineer*.
William Chalmers, *George Mercer Dawson: Geologist, Scientist, Explorer*.
Anne Cimon, *Susanna Moodie: Pioneer Author*.
Deborah Cowley, *Lucille Teasdale: Doctor of Courage*.
Gary Evans, *John Grierson: Trailblazer of Documentary Film*.
Judith Fitzgerald, *Marshall McLuhan: Wise Guy*.
lian goodall, *William Lyon Mackenzie King: Dreams and Shadows*.
Stephen Eaton Hume, *Frederick Banting: Hero, Healer, Artist*.
Naïm Kattan, *A.M. Klein: Poet and Prophet*.
Betty Keller, *Pauline Johnson: First Aboriginal Voice of Canada*.
Heather Kirk, *Mazo de la Roche: Rich and Famous Writer*.
Michelle Labrèche-Larouche, *Emma Albani: International Star*.
Wayne Larsen, *A.Y. Jackson: A Love for the Land*.
Francine Legaré, *Samuel de Champlain: Father of New France*.
Margaret Macpherson, *Nellie McClung: Voice for the Voiceless*.
Dave Margoshes, *Tommy Douglas: Building the New Society*.
Marguerite Paulin, *René Lévesque: Charismatic Leader*.
Marguerite Paulin, *Maurice Duplessis: Powerbroker, Politician*.
Raymond Plante, *Jacques Plante: Behind the Mask*.
T.F. Rigelhof, *George Grant: Redefining Canada*.
Arthur Slade, *John Diefenbaker: An Appointment with Destiny*.
Roderick Stewart, *Wilfrid Laurier: A Pledge for Canada*.
John Wilson, *John Franklin: Traveller on Undiscovered Seas*.
John Wilson, *Norman Bethune: A Life of Passionate Conviction*.
Rachel Wyatt, *Agnes Macphail: Champion of the Underdog*.

Mazo de la Roche

Library and Archives Canada Cataloguing in Publication
Kirk, Heather, 1949-

  Mazo de la Roche: rich and famous writer

  (The Quest library ; 27)
  Includes bibliographical references and index.
  ISBN-13: 978-1-894852-20-3
  ISBN-10: 1-894852-20-6

  1. De la Roche, Mazo, 1879-1961. 2. Authors, Canadian (English) – 20th century – Biography. I. Title. II. Series: Quest library; 27.

PS8507.E43Z74 2006   C813'.52   C2006-941159-X
PS9507.E43Z74 2006

Legal Deposit: Third quarter 2006
Library and Archives Canada
Bibliothèque et Achives nationales du Québec

XYZ Publishing acknowledges the support of The Quest Library project by the Book Publishing Industry Development Program (BPIDP) of the Department of Canadian Heritage. The opinions expressed do not necessarily reflect the views of the Government of Canada.

The publishers further acknowledge the financial support our publishing program receives from The Canada Council for the Arts, the ministère de la Culture et des Communications du Québec, and the Société de développement des entreprises culturelles.

Chronology: Clarence Karr
Index: Darcy Dunton
Layout: Édiscript enr.
Cover design: Zirval Design
Cover illustration: Magali Lefrançois
Photo research: Heather Kirk
Mazo de la Roche signature: courtesy Kate Barlow

Printed and bound in Canada

XYZ Publishing   Distributed by: University of Toronto Press Distribution
1781 Saint Hubert Street   5201 Dufferin Street
Montreal, Quebec H2L 3Z1   Toronto, ON, M3H 5T8
Tel: (514) 525-2170   Tel: 416-667-7791; Toll-free: 800-565-9523
Fax: (514) 525-7537   Fax: 416-667-7832; Toll-free: 800-221-9985
E-mail: info@xyzedit.qc.ca   E-mail: utpbooks@utpress.utoronto.ca
Web site: www.xyzedit.qc.ca   Web site: utpress.utoronto.ca
International Rights: Contact André Vanasse, tel. (514) 525-2170 # 25
                    E-mail: andre.vanasse@xyzedit.qc.ca

de la ROCHE

Mazo

RICH AND FAMOUS WRITER

For Clara Thomas,
a pioneer in Canadian literary biography

Contents

Mazo de la Roche and Bunty on the front page of the Toronto *Star*, April 1927, after winning the $10,0000 *Atlantic Monthly*-Little, Brown Award.

Prologue

Mazo carried Bunty, the blind, old, black Scottish terrier, down to the little back garden to do her business. The snow had melted and little green shoots were poking out of the cold dark earth. Mazo carried Bunty back up again to the stuffy, rented, third-floor flat. Mazo, Caroline, and Bunty ate their breakfast, then Caroline left for work the way she always did.

While Bunty sat beside the rocking chair and listened, Mazo perched herself again today on the window seat and watched the sidewalk that led to the front door. When the postman came, Mazo ignored Bunty, flew down the stairs, and fetched the mail.

"Nothing from the writing competition," Mazo said to Bunty as she returned to the flat. "One of the other manuscripts has been chosen, I suppose. *Jalna* has been thrust aside and forgotten."

Bunty cocked her head.

Finally Mazo fetched the pages she had been working on and sat down in the rocker with the pages resting on a drawing board in her lap. She began to rock.

She rocked and rocked, but no words came.

"What's the use?" Mazo muttered bitterly.

But then Mazo looked at Bunty.

"I shall be there," the grizzled dog seemed to say. "I am the centre of all this."

"You do your best to understand our life, don't you!" exclaimed Mazo. "You give your staunch spirit to us."

Through twelve difficult years, Bunty had guided Mazo. Or so Mazo felt.

Mazo stopped rocking, put her feet up on the two bulky volumes of Dr. Johnson's *Dictionary*, and began to scribble with a pencil in a squarish, strong handwriting.

She was working on her fifth novel. It would be a sequel to her fourth, *Jalna*, which she had entered in an international competition. She didn't have a title for the sequel yet, but the story was coming along well. It too was about a big family like the one she had grown up in, except this family was rich – at least the grandmother was.

In the sequel to *Jalna*, Gran Whiteoak would die and leave her fortune to one of her sons or grandsons. Which one?

Sometimes Mazo imagined she was Gran Whiteoak. Sometimes she imagined she was one of the sons or grandsons. Today she was Gran...

Bunty curled up beside a radiator and sighed. She knew several hours would pass before Mazo would be ready to go for a walk through the fascinating streets of the big-city neighbourhood where they had spent the winter. Until those hours had passed, Mazo would rock, pause, write, consult the dictionary, rock, pause, and write again.

Bunty slept.

∞

"*Jalna* has won the competition!" Mazo blurted immediately to Caroline when the latter returned home from the office. "A telegram came."

Mazo thrust the telegram at Caroline.

In a daze Caroline read the words: "Have patience. Happy news awaits you."

"Oh," Caroline said flatly. Then she sat down and looked blankly at Mazo. Caroline Louise Clement was past rejoicing. She had suffered suspense too long.

Mazo's enthusiasm evaporated. She sat down too, and both women remained silent for a long time.

"When we do feel any emotion about this, we'll have to dam it up," remarked Mazo finally. "The publishers asked me not to tell anyone about my win until they notify the press. It will be about ten days. But of course I had to tell *you*."

"Perhaps we should leave town," suggested Caroline. "It might be easier. We could rest, collect ourselves, and prepare for the publicity. Let's go to Niagara Falls."

"Publicity. I'd forgotten about that," moaned Mazo. "I think I already feel sick."

Caroline and Mazo were cousins, but they were as close as sisters and always worked as a team. Caroline was well aware that Mazo feared new people and situations.

"Shall we take Bunty?" asked Caroline, changing the subject. "Travelling is so hard on her now."

Bunty wagged her stubby, curved tail.

"We must," replied Mazo. "Remember how she swam after the canoe when we tried to leave her while we went to get supplies?"

"Remember how she jumped onto the seat of the van when we had to move again?" asked Caroline.

"Yes," agreed Mazo. "She was courageous then, as always."

∞

"TORONTO WOMAN WINS $10,000 ATLANTIC MONTHLY NOVEL PRIZE" was the caption below the front-page photo of Mazo and Bunty in the Toronto *Star* of Monday, April 11, 1927. Overnight, Mazo had become a rich and famous writer. Her telephone and doorbell rang all day. Messenger boys arrived with telegrams of congratulations. Florists' boxes arrived containing every kind of flower. Reporters arrived to interview her. Friends arrived to congratulate her. The partying went on for months.

Novelists from all around the world had entered their work in an American competition for best novel, and a Canadian – Mazo de la Roche – had won!

Mazo's big win after many years of financial and personal struggle was wonderful, but it was not to be her only triumph. She would go on to write sixteen novels about a Canadian family called the Whiteoaks living in a house called Jalna, and these novels would sell in the millions in many languages and many countries. Her Jalna novels would be made into a Hollywood movie and a Broadway play. This same play, *Whiteoaks*, would be the first Canadian play to be mounted on a professional stage in London, England. And it was a hit!

Mazo would write other books too, and she would win more awards. She would live in a mansion next door to the king and queen of England. She would become one of Canada's most popular authors ever.

Mazo de la Roche at two years.

1

Beginnings

I was not born where I should have been, in my father's house, but in my grandfather's.

When she heard the distant whistle of the early-morning freight train, Mazo gazed down the long, terraced hill toward the railway tracks below and assumed her racer's crouch.

There was the train! Almost even with the edge of the lawn where she waited, the locomotive shrieked its challenge. Mazo shrieked hers. They were off!

Her long auburn hair flying, Mazo raced the train to the opposite end of the lawn.

She won! As always! And today the painted symbol on the boxcar just behind the locomotive was a full moon!

"A fine day, Grandma!" shouted Mazo as she ran toward the back door of the solid, two-storey, red-brick house. "It was a full moon, so it's going to be a fine day."

Inside the house a short, bright-eyed woman with wavy grey hair pulled back into a neat bun was already busy baking, despite the early hour. She smiled warmly as her cherished only grandchild entered the kitchen.

"My, you're a big help," said Grandma Lundy. "And you're just five years old, the same age as my little sister Martha was when we moved to Cherry Creek. Martha didn't have to help Mother. But I did. Of course I was a big girl of nine. I had no time to play. I had chores to do."

"Chores are too much work," commented Mazo, dancing around the room.

"That's just how I felt!" exclaimed Grandma Lundy. "Why, I had to help my mother in the kitchen and the garden. I fed the chickens too. And I minded little Martha and baby Mary. We were pioneering in the primeval forest. My father and big brothers, Wellington and Lambert, were chopping down trees to make fields. There was so much to do, everyone had to help."

"I don't like helping," said Mazo.

"You may say that now," said Grandma Lundy. "But I could not. I had to help."

"Tell me about how there was Willsons' Hill and Clements' Hill in Cherry Creek," said Mazo. "Tell me how your little sister Martha married James Clement whose father was so rich."

"You go and play, Mazo," said Grandma Lundy. "I have work to do. I must bake four loaves of bread and two rhubarb pies."

"There's no one to play with," said Mazo. "Father is in Toronto, Mother is sick in bed, Aunt Eva is dusting the sitting room so it will look nice when her gentleman-caller comes, Uncle Frank is working with Grandpa at the factory, Uncle George is working at the post office, Uncle Walter is at school, and Chub is outside barking at something."

"Your father will visit in a few days, and he will take you back with him to Toronto," said Grandma Lundy.

"I want somebody to play with now," said Mazo.

"Since it is going to be a fine day, you and Grandpa and I will go for a drive in the buggy this afternoon. We must go and see my brother Wellington. He and his family don't know their neighbours very well yet because they just moved from Cherry Creek last year, so Grandpa's going to help with some carpentry work and I'm going to bring some baking."

"Can we stop and see Grandpa's Grandpa's house?" asked Mazo.

"We can if you're good," said Grandma Lundy. "Now go read your storybook."

Mazo de la Roche was born on January 15, 1879 in the village of Newmarket, York County, Ontario, in the home of her mother's parents, Daniel and Louise Lundy. She was named Mazo Louise Roche. Her father, William Richmond Roche, gave Mazo her unusual first name. "Mazo" was supposedly the name of a girl Will Roche had once known and liked.

A few weeks after Mazo was born, Daniel Ambrose Lundy borrowed money to buy a house on Prospect Street in Newmarket. Most of Mazo's first nine years of life were spent in this house, which still stands today. The house looked down at the Northern Railway tracks and across at the Main Street of Newmarket, population two thousand.

But Mazo spent summer vacations in the old Cherry Creek district at the south end of Innisfil Township, Simcoe County, about twenty kilometres north of Newmarket. Innisfil Township was where some of her Grandma Lundy's nearest relatives lived, and where there was a nice lake to swim in: Lake Simcoe. Sometimes Mazo also visited her father's family in Newmarket or, between 1884 and 1889, in Toronto.

Daniel and Louise Lundy were like parents for Mazo because her real parents, William and Alberta Roche, did not have their own home. Besides, Alberta was ill and could not run a household or raise a child. Alberta, or "Bertie," was a pretty woman with gingery light-brown hair and violet eyes, and she loved pretty clothes. Bertie had been healthy when she married the dark-haired, dark-eyed Will Roche, who was tall and handsome, and who danced and talked charmingly. But Bertie caught scarlet fever when she was about to give birth to her first and only child, Mazo, and the ravages of the disease left her an invalid for decades.

Daniel and Louise (Willson) Lundy were the grandchildren of Quaker immigrants from the United States. These immigrants had come to Canada between about 1800 and 1810 and had cleared farms from the forest near Newmarket. Later, about 1840, Louise Lundy's immediate family, the Willsons, had moved to Cherry Creek. When they grew up, Daniel and Louise Lundy became Methodists, as did many Quakers of their time and place.

Grandpa Lundy was a skilled worker and a natural leader. He was foreman of the William Cane woodenware factory in Newmarket. He designed and supervised the creation of the machinery used in the factory, and he also supervised the building of Newmarket's town hall.

Mazo loved her Grandpa Lundy. He had thick silvery hair and blue eyes, and he was tall and strong. He was fun. He was kind and generous with his family and friends, and although he often got angry, he never got angry with Mazo.

The Lundy home was already crowded when newborn Mazo joined it. There were Grandpa and Grandma Lundy, of course, plus four adult children and one six-year-old boy. Sometimes too Mazo's father came and stayed with the Lundys.

Although Mazo lived with a confusing crowd of close relatives, she was often lonely because none of these relatives were her own age. She sought companionship in stories, and she could be very affected by what she heard or read.

Once, when Mazo was very young, a much older child who lived nearby told her a ghost story about a woman with a golden arm. According to the story, the woman died and her husband sold her arm. But the woman haunted her husband, and moaned, "Bring me back my golden arm! Bring me back my golden arm!"

That night, Mazo lay awake in her bed with her hands over her ears and listened to the dead woman moan, "Bring me back my golden arm!" The ghost came closer and closer, past the stuffed owl on the stairs, closer and closer... Mazo jumped out of bed and fled down the stairs to the lit-up sitting room where the adults sat playing cards cheerfully. Soon she was safe in her father's arms, and Grandpa Lundy was raging against the older child.

Mazo created her own little imagined world. Her playmates were made-up characters. And from the very beginning she was sensitive to words. As a baby, she had refused to talk baby talk. She always spoke clearly. Later, she often invented words such as *beckittybock* for petticoat, *gillygaws* for socks, and *conehat* for jacket.

At an early age she began to read. Soon she was devouring books voraciously, reading the Kate Greenaway books, *Alice in Wonderland*, *Through the Looking Glass*, *The Water Babies*, and *The Little Duke*. She also read old issues of magazines for boys, like *The Boys' Own* and *Chum*, that she found in the attic of the Lundy home.

∞

The well-fed, muscular horse trotted smartly along the narrow dirt road flanked by massive oak trees. The sun shone, the birds sang, and the new green leaves rustled. Mazo, wedged comfortably between Grandpa and Grandma Lundy on the driver's seat of the buggy, was thoroughly enjoying this excursion in the country on a fine spring day.

Finally Mazo spotted the stately, two-story, red-brick house on a hill. Mazo loved this house. This was Grandpa's Grandpa's house. Grandpa Lundy slowed the horse.

"Grandpa, were you born in your Grandpa's house like I was born in your house?" asked Mazo, gazing at the handsome house, the big wooden barn, the blossoming orchard, and the moist, dark fields.

"I was born on the neighbouring farm where my brother Shadrack Lundy lives now," said Grandpa Lundy. "When I was born, my Grandpa Lundy was still building the red-brick house. He finished it the next year. When I was your age, I spent many hours in this house, visiting my grandparents and playing with my cousins. It was a dark day last year when Cousin Silas Lundy sold our grandfather's farm out of the family."

"Did your grandfather have a thousand acres of land, Grandpa?" asked Mazo.

"Oh no, that was my great-great-great grandfather, Richard Lundy," said Grandpa Lundy. "My grandfather, Enos Lundy Senior, owned only four hundred acres. And my father, Enos Lundy Junior, owned only one hundred acres. Richard Lundy received his land from the great William Penn himself. One thousand acres of primeval forest in Bucks County, Pennsylvania."

"Did Richard Lundy come from the States up the Walnut Trail in a wagon?" asked Mazo.

"That was Enos Lundy Senior," said Grandpa Lundy. "Richard Lundy came over the sea from England in a big sailing ship and founded our proud Lundy family in America. Why, the cow path where the Battle of Lundy's Lane took place was named after my

Grandpa Lundy's first cousin, William Lundy, who owned a farm nearby. That was in the War of 1812."

"Having a cow path named after you is nothing to be proud of," sniffed Grandma Lundy.

"Another of Grandpa's first cousins, Benjamin Lundy, was a pioneer abolitionist who wrote about the need to free the black slaves of America," said Grandpa Lundy.

"I thought the Lundys were knights in the olden days," said Mazo.

"That's the Bostwicks," said Grandpa Lundy. "My mother was a Bostwick. The Bostwicks were United Empire Loyalists in Nova Scotia, and knights back in old England. Now my mother's mother – my Grandma Bostwick – was a Lardner. Grandma's uncle, Nathaniel Lardner, was a famous biblical scholar in England. Her son, Lardner Bostwick, was one of Toronto's first aldermen – he sat on the council with William Lyon Mackenzie. I remember when Grandma Bostwick got word that Uncle Lardner had died of the cholera plague in Toronto in 1834. She took the news awful hard. You see, Grandma Bostwick lived in Grandpa Lundy's red-brick house too, because Uncle Isaac Lundy had married Aunt Keziah Bostwick…"

"Families are awfully confusing, Grandpa," said Mazo, swinging her legs.

ༀ

Mazo's father, William Roche, worked for his brother, Danford Roche. By 1884, Danford Roche had stores in Barrie, Newmarket, Aurora, and Toronto. At the age of five, Mazo began to go by train occasionally to visit her father and his family in Toronto.

Toronto streets were not quiet like country roads. Horses, horses, everywhere! A team of powerful draft horses pulled a dray. A skinny horse pulled a butcher's cart. Elegant horses pulled an elegant carriage. People everywhere! Women in their long flounced skirts. Men who looked like gentlemen. An Italian boy pushed his barrow of bananas and called, "Ban-ana ripe, fifteen cents a dozen!" The bananas were red.

The inside of Grandmother Roche's house in downtown Toronto was dim and forbidding. Mazo held her father's hand as they climbed the long, thickly carpeted stairway to Grandmother Roche's mother's room. Great-grandmother Bryan was ninety-two years old. She was dying! She was lying in the middle of a vast, four-poster bed.

"My little darling!" the old woman exclaimed in a surprisingly strong voice with a thick Irish accent. She reached out her long arms for Mazo. Great-grandmother Bryan was still charming, demonstrative, and domineering – an irresistible force!

Great-grandmother Bryan was Mazo's father's grandmother, and he loved his grandmother more than he loved his mother.

Will Roche lifted Mazo up so she could kiss Great-grandmother Bryan.

When the old woman hugged her closely, Mazo was afraid. She was grateful when her father rescued her. She clasped his neck tightly as he carried her down the stairs.

Around the table at dinner that day were red-haired and hot-tempered Uncle Danford; prim and proper Aunty Ida; calm and peace-loving Grandmother Roche; and black-haired and studious Uncle Francis. Mazo sat beside her father, and watched and listened.

"What was Father really like, Mother?" asked Uncle Francis. "Dan and Will were old enough to know him. But I…"

"Your father was not a common sort of man," said Grandmother Roche. Mazo was impressed by the dignity of Grandmother Roche's appearance. Her long waist was encased in a black bodice with white ruching at the neck and wrists. Around her neck was a long gold chain. Great-grandmother Bryan had given her that chain for being a good daughter.

"Mr. John Roche may have been descended from the aristocratic *de la Roche* clan of old France, but he was a rotter," said Uncle Danford, who was standing at the head of the table carving a huge roast of beef. Aunty Ida was serving the potatoes, vegetables, and gravy.

"Your father left us to find a teaching position that suited him," said Grandmother Roche.

"I know that, Mother, but what was he like? I mean his personality," persisted Francis.

"I tell you he was a rotter," insisted Danford, putting a generous slice of roast beef on his mother's plate. "He never earned enough income to support a family. Mother had to work as a milliner. He deserted his wife and sons. Grandmother Bryan forbade Mother to follow him. But unfortunately Mother visited him once and conceived you. Fortunately Grandfather

Bryan left us some property when he died, so we weren't completely destitute. "

"Now Danny, your father was a brilliant scholar," said Grandmother Roche. "You should be proud of him."

"Oh yes, he was always planning reading courses for us, and sending us presents of books in French, Latin, and Greek," said Mazo's father. "And he corrected our grammar."

"It was a mild spring morning and beginning to rain," said Grandmother Roche, ignoring her full plate of steaming food. "I had just bought myself a new bonnet, trimmed with flowers and a satin bow. Little sister Fanny, who was then eight, was carrying the bonnet box. We came out of the milliner's and were confronted by the shower. What were we to do? Return to the shop, when our mother expected us home? Never – we must face the rain.

"Just then a young man appeared before us – not only appeared but offered us the shelter of his umbrella! He bowed as he offered it. He spoke very correctly. And his looks! Why they fairly took my breath away! He was six feet tall, and stalwart. He was smooth shaven – that was unusual in those days. As for his clothes – never had I seen such elegance. His top hat was worn at just the right angle. His coat was dark blue with silver buttons. His cravat – I have no words fine enough to describe his cravat."

"Eat up, Mother," muttered Uncle Danford. "Your dinner will be cold."

∞

In 1826, Great-grandmother Bryan had emigrated from Ireland to Canada with her husband and children. Eventually the Bryans had settled in Whitby, where Great-grandfather Bryan worked as a shoemaker. The five Bryan boys mostly became tinsmiths or businessmen, although one, Jacob, became Whitby's chief of police. The oldest of the three Bryan girls, Sarah, married John Roche. John Richmond Roche, M.A., was a fellow immigrant from Ireland and a teacher.

The Bryans hated John Roche. They were Methodists; he was Catholic. They were down-to-earth; he was high-faluting. They stuck together; he was a loner. Sarah's marriage to John Roche did not last long. John Roche went to the United States by himself. Eventually he became a professor of mathematics at Newton University in Baltimore, Maryland.

In 1876, easy-going Will Roche, middle son of John and Sarah Roche, had come from Whitby, fifty kilometres east of Toronto, to Newmarket, fifty kilometres north, in order to help his older brother Danford. Danford Roche had just bought his first store. The store was on Main Street in Newmarket. His establishment, a general and dry-goods store, was called "The Leading House."

Will soon married Bertie Lundy. Danford married Ida Pearson. Danford and Ida Roche never had children. Mazo was the only grandchild on her father's side of the family too.

In 1880, despite his hatred of his father, Danford Roche had gone during hot July weather to fetch the body of Grandfather Roche from Baltimore to Newmarket for burial. At the age of sixty-six

Grandfather Roche had dropped dead of sunstroke on the street in front of his boarding house. Uncle Danford had also fetched home twenty-eight boxes of Grandfather Roche's expensive books. Uncle Danford had put the boxes in his stable in Newmarket. He had no room for them in his house. The books were great classics of literature. For a long time only Uncle Francis read the books. Much later Mazo read some of them too.

In 1884, Danford Roche bought a store on Yonge Street in Toronto, and his mother bought a house on John Street in Toronto. Now Will Roche was helping in the Toronto store, working variously as a clerk, manager, and cloth cutter. Danford had located his Toronto store next door to a similar establishment owned by Timothy Eaton. Danford was very competitive!

⌒

Mazo adored her father, and she found Grandfather Roche fascinating. Still, she was glad when the time came to go to Toronto's Union Station and board the train back to Newmarket. Soon Mazo was allowed to ride the train herself. Off she went, in the conductor's care, back to Grandpa and Grandma Lundy. She was not nervous, for the train was her friend.

The next morning, Mazo and the train raced again in the wind. Today on the first freight car there was a crescent moon. Mazo ran back to the house, into the room where Grandma Lundy was sewing.

"Bad weather, Grandma," Mazo announced. "Thunderstorms!"

Mazo de la Roche at eleven years.

2

No Longer Lonely

"This is Caroline," my grandmother said to me. "You two little girls must be friends."

When Caroline saw that Winnipeg was behind them and the long train was clacking faster and faster past flat, snow-covered prairie and bare aspen trees, she sighed, sat down, and began swinging her short legs back and forth restlessly.

The view out the window was boring again, like the view from Grand Forks to Winnipeg. Caroline hadn't seen a single buffalo in the whole Dakota Territory. The Red River had been frozen and grey. The Pembina Mountains had been stupid hills.

"When will there be the forests and lakes in Ontario?" Caroline asked her mother.

"Tomorrow," said her mother, pulling their lunch out of a bundle.

"Will Father be alone at Christmas?" asked Caroline, frowning.

"Serves him right if he is," said her mother. "Now you eat your bread and cheese."

Caroline ignored her sandwich and looked around the inside of the passenger car. It was early December 1886 and the car was crowded with Canadian families going Back East for the winter. Some were eating a cold meal. Others were playing cards. Still others were making beds for the little children who needed a nap... The seats were made of wooden slats. Above the seats were shelves that pulled down so they hung by rods and hinges.

Am I going to sleep on a shelf? Caroline asked herself. *No! Never! I am eight years old!*

At one end of the car were the washrooms. At the other end was a room with a stove to cook on. There was water at that end too. Everybody had to share. Caroline did not like sharing.

"How long will we be on this train?" asked Caroline.

"Two or three days," said her mother.

"Why does the trip take so long?"

"Because we're going almost as far as Toronto. We'll get off the train in Cherry Creek, and Uncle Lambert will meet us. I wrote him a letter and told him we were coming."

"Did you tell him I can recite, 'The Jackdaw of Rheims'?"

"Yes. And I said you could read well and sew beautifully."

"I was born in Uncle Lambert's house, wasn't I?"

"Yes. Uncle Lambert's house is near Aunt Mary's house in Cherry Creek. Lambert is my older brother, and Mary is my younger sister. Cherry Creek is where your father and I grew up. In Cherry Creek there was Willsons' Hill and Clements' Hill..."

"Did it take three days for us to go Out West and join Father in Grand Forks?"

"Oh no! It took much longer than that! About one week. The Canadian Pacific Railroad was just finished this year. Seven years ago we had to go through the United States to reach Grand Forks. We took the train from Lefroy to Toronto, Toronto to Sarnia, Sarnia to Chicago, Chicago to St. Paul, St. Paul to Grand Forks."

"Are we going to borrow money from our relatives Back East?"

"Certainly not! And don't you mention one single thing about our problems to one single soul!"

"I won't," said Caroline. She bit into her sandwich angrily.

Mazo supposed her eighth birthday, on January 15, would be as gloomy as Christmas and New Year's Day had been. Grandpa and Grandma Lundy were still terribly sad about Uncle Frank. Everyone was. Mazo's mother said everyone should stay in Newmarket until after January 14, so Grandpa and Grandma wouldn't have to face the first anniversary of Uncle Frank's tragic death alone.

Uncle Frank's head had been cut off by a saw! "No blame whatever can be attached to anyone for the sad occurrence," the newspaper had said. "It was purely accidental." The terrible tragedy had happened on the day before Mazo's seventh birthday!

Uncle Frank's death was why Mazo's father and her Uncle George Lundy had not gone back to Toronto yet. Instead they had gone somewhere in the horse-drawn sleigh through the snow on an errand, and they had come back with a big bundle.

Uncle George sat down in Grandpa Lundy's armchair and began to remove layer after layer of shawls from the bundle on his lap. The adults stood about, waiting and watching. None of them took any notice of Mazo, who hung back. From the top of the bundle hung strands of silvery fair hair like the limp petals of a flower. There was a child in the bundle! A girl!

The girl stared about her. She looked dazed. Her hair hung down to her shoulders, but it was cut squarely into a straight thick fringe above her blue eyes. She had high cheekbones, a square little chin and full curling lips. She looked as though she would never, ever smile again.

Mazo's mother and Aunt Eva asked the girl all sorts of questions about where she had been and what she had seen.

The girl answered every question with only two words: "Yes, ma'am" or "No, ma'am."

"Listen to her!" exclaimed Aunt Eva. "Why, she's a real little American!"

"I think you and Caroline had better go off and get acquainted, Mazo," said Grandma Lundy. "Tea will be ready soon. Caroline must be starving."

Uncle George set the girl on her feet. She came and put her hand into Mazo's.

Mazo led Caroline into the red-carpeted sitting room and showed her where the Christmas tree had stood touching the ceiling. Then Mazo started up the stairs to show Caroline her favourite book, *Through the Looking Glass*. Halfway up the stairs, Mazo and Caroline stopped where the stuffed white owl sat in a recess in the wall.

"He's pretty," said Caroline. She let go of Mazo's hand, stood on tiptoe, and put both her hands underneath its wings.

"He was alive once," said Mazo, who was afraid of the owl. "He flew around in the woods and killed things. He was wicked. At night he comes down and flies all over the house and hoots. I've heard him."

"Ah ha ha ha!" laughed Caroline merrily, and she scampered up the stairs.

Mazo, astonished that Caroline was not afraid, ran after her.

Chub, the fox terrier, barked and came running too.

∞

As far as young Mazo was concerned, Caroline Clement came into her life like a white rabbit pops out of a black top hat: by magic. One day Caroline simply appeared. Presto! There she was! Mazo's father and uncle had brought the girl from some relatives who didn't like children. But in fact Caroline's arrival at the Lundy house in Newmarket was the result of many years of money problems due to the restless seeking of Caroline's father: James Clement.

For Caroline's mother, Martha (Willson) Clement, the family finances had been a worry in the West as well as the East. When Martha had married James Clement in the early 1850s, he had owned a forty-hectare farm in Cherry Creek just a kilometre or two from the Willsons. James Clement had got his farm for 150 dollars from his wealthy father, Lewis James Clement, who owned more than 400 hectares of land in Innisfil Township. James wanted to raise show horses and show them in New York State.

But James had sold this farm and bought another farm nearby that was not cleared and had no house. James and Martha had lived over the store across the road from the farm, and James had managed the store. Then James had sold his second farm to pay some debts. After that, James and Martha and their first two children had lived in hotels in Bell Ewart and Bracebridge while James had managed the hotels. Then, in the summer of 1877, James had left Martha and the children with Grandmother Willson in Innisfil Township and travelled to the American West to scout new opportunities. After James was gone, Martha realized she was pregnant.

The baby, Caroline Louise, was born April 4, 1878. One year later, Martha, eight-year-old Mary Elizabeth, five-year-old James Harvey, and baby Caroline joined James in the Dakota Territory. In booming Grand Forks, James found plenty of work as a carpenter, and in 1882 he managed to purchase a sixty-five-hectare property on the edge of town by borrowing six hundred dollars: a large sum of money at that time. The family seemed settled at last.

But in 1883 – the same year that Mary Elizabeth died – James borrowed another large sum of money to capitalize on an invention he had patented: a ditch-digging machine. Unfortunately, this business scheme failed. In the summer of 1885, the sheriff seized James's property and auctioned it to the highest bidder in front of the court house in Grand Forks. Now Martha, James, and their surviving children were living in a rented house, and James wasn't able to pay the rent.

In December 1886, Martha Clement and two children boarded a Winnipeg-bound train in Grand Forks. Martha needed to see her family. Back in Cherry Creek, after the hot Christmas dinners had been digested and the warmly remembered relatives had been visited, the chill reality of Martha Clement's difficult position set in. Where was the penniless woman to spend the winter? Where were her children to stay?

The many brothers and sisters of Martha and James Clement had their own families to support. Their houses were mostly full. They had their own problems to deal with…

Thankfully, Martha's sister, Louise (Willson) Lundy, who lived just a short train-ride away in Newmarket, felt that the two little female cousins, Caroline and Mazo, just nine months apart, would get along fine and be less trouble than one. They did and they were.

When Martha Clement boarded a westbound CPR train and went back to Grand Forks that spring, she took her son but left Caroline behind. During the next three years, Caroline flourished under the loving care of her Aunt Louise.

The two little girls came together like two drops of water. It was just as though they had always been together, they were so completely companionable, so completely seemed to fill each other's needs. Most of the time they lived in an imagined world of Mazo's making.

Mazo had created this world when she did not have a child her own age to play with, and now she shared it with Caroline. Caroline couldn't create, but she could follow. She was wonderful at following the creator, and at imagining! She could imagine herself anything at all, and that of course helped Mazo's imagination greatly. Any situation that Mazo imagined, Caroline was in it, heart and soul.

As time went on, Mazo and Caroline introduced more and more characters into their imagined world. They added old people, middle-aged people, babies, upper-class people, lower-class people, priests, schoolboys, engineers, maids, actresses, horses, and dogs. More than a hundred characters! As Mazo and Caroline got to know the characters better, they ceased to act them. They *were* them. When surrounded by other people, they strained toward the moment when they could be alone together. Then, at once, the real world became unreal. The vivid reality was their play.

The girls carried their imagined world with them when they moved in 1888 with the Lundys to Orillia, a small town in Simcoe County, about one hundred kilometres north of Newmarket. Daniel Lundy could not bear to continue working in the factory where his son, Frank, had been killed, so he accepted a position as foreman of the Thompson brothers' woodenware factory in Orillia. Today Orillians call it the Old Pail Factory.

In Orillia, Mazo and Caroline were the youngest in a household that included Mazo's mother, Bertie, as well as Aunt Eva, Uncle Walter, and Grandpa and Grandma Lundy. Will Roche still joined the Lundy household occasionally, and Bertie and Mazo joined Will occasionally in his rented rooms in Toronto.

Will was no longer working for his older brother. Danford Roche's Toronto store had failed, and his mercantile empire had collapsed. Uncle Danford had retreated to Newmarket and gone into business with a relative of his wife. Grandmother Roche had sold her house in Toronto to redeem Danford's credit, and she too had retreated to Newmarket. Will now worked at a variety of jobs. For example, he was both a traveller for a wholesale grocer and the treasurer of a civic spectacle in Toronto called, "The Cyclorama of the Battle of Sedan."

In the summers, the family made one-day excursions by ferry from Orillia to tiny Strawberry Island in Lake Simcoe, where Mazo and Caroline imagined they were Robinson Crusoe and Friday in a cave. The family also went on longer excursions to Cherry Creek, where they stayed in a little cottage by Lake Simcoe. In those days there were no cars or speedboats. The summer cottages were few and they were surrounded by farmlands. One summer, Mazo's mother, Caroline, and Mazo all had matching, blue-flannel bathing dresses trimmed with white braid.

During the rest of the year, Mazo and Caroline studied in a little private school run by Miss Cecile Lafferty, later Mrs. Gerhardt Dryer, wife of Orillia's chief of police. The school was located on Coldwater Road, not far from where the Lundys lived. Outside of school the girls enjoyed recreational reading like *Little Women* by Louisa May Alcott. In the fall and spring they took long walks and played the usual childhood games, like hide-and-seek. In the winter they skated. Mittened hands held mittened hands as a dozen children did a crack-the-whip across the rink. Mazo's and Caroline's skates never fit right, and their flannel petticoats always got in the way.

Now and then Mazo and Caroline tried acting as well as imagining. The two girls, in costume, would act out plays for their family. As well, the girls tried writing a newspaper that contained stories, verses, riddles, and news. They printed the newspaper by hand and sold it to the family for two cents a copy. Perhaps the price was too high, for the newspaper did not last long.

∞

Mazo, seated at the kitchen table, wrote on and on. While Grandma Lundy kneaded the bread dough and made an apple pie, Mazo covered eight whole, foolscap pages!

"What are you writing, Mazo?" asked Grandma Lundy.

"A story," Mazo replied without looking up. She kept on writing.

"*Youth's Companion* is advertising a short-story competition for children of sixteen and under," said Mazo's mother, entering the kitchen with Caroline. "Mazo thinks she can win."

"It's a story about a lost child named Nancy," said Caroline.

"But Mazo is only ten," said Grandma. "She can't compete with sixteen-year-olds."

"There! It's finished," announced Mazo, putting down her pen and gathering up the pages. "Nancy went through terrible times. She was forced to eat potato peels. But at last she was restored to her mother. And her mother quoted St. Luke, Grandma. When Nancy came home, her mother said: 'It was meet that we should make merry, and be glad: thy brother was dead, and is alive again; and was lost, and is found.'"

"But darling," said Mazo's mother, "do you think a child would ever be so hungry she would eat potato peels?"

"Nancy was," Mazo said firmly.

"And do you think her mother would quote a Bible text the moment her child was given back to her?" asked Mazo's mother. "It sounds so pompous!"

This criticism Mazo could not answer. She stared down at the pages in her hands.

"I'm dead sure I'd eat potato peels if I were hungry enough," came the voice of Mazo's father from behind her. "And as for the text – it was the proper thing for the mother to quote. Don't change a word of your story, Mazo. It will probably win the prize."

Two weeks later, Mazo received a long envelope in the mail. Inside was her story. It had not won the competition. Also inside was a letter from the editor of *Youth's Companion*. It said: "If the promise shown by this story is fulfilled, you will make a good writer yet."

"Isn't that splendid!" exclaimed Mazo's mother.

Mazo sat on a stool in a corner, covered her face with her hands, and sobbed out her disappointment. Her family, not knowing what to say, stood around her for a long time.

Finally her father spoke.

"Come on, Mazo," he said. "I'm going to teach you how to play cribbage. It's a good game, and you have no idea how comforting a game of cards can be."

∽

In 1889, Caroline's parents and older brother arrived in Orillia. The reunion was not happy because Caroline's father was not happy. James Clement was a poor man who could barely afford to rent a few small rooms to shelter his family. He and his teenage son were working at menial jobs in the pail factory where his brother-in-law, Daniel Lundy, was the foreman. Daniel Lundy – Mazo's Grandpa Lundy – had given the jobs to James and his son.

James still owned about twenty hectares of land in Cherry Creek that had been willed him by his father. But he could not make a living from this land, and he could not sell it. Grandfather Clement's will stated that the land must go to James's children after James died. Anyway, James didn't want to live near his family in Cherry Creek. His family scorned him.

All of his brothers and sisters had done better than he had! Stephen was sheriff of the entire western judicial district of Manitoba. Sarah and her husband had a farm in Manitoba. Lewis was a medical doctor in Bradford, Ontario. Catherine's husband had been a successful merchant in Barrie, Ontario; furthermore, he had represented the riding of North Simcoe in the Parliament in Ottawa for nine years. Even Joseph, David, and Eliza, who never left Cherry Creek, at least owned forty or more hectares of land there. What was wrong with James?

James was a traitor! He had forsaken queen and country! He had become an American citizen! Although the Clements were of French, Dutch, and German descent, they had been officers in the British army for four generations. They had been United Empire Loyalists, pioneers of Niagara, heroes of the War of 1812. They had fought *against* the Americans. James's grandfather had been killed in that war! James was the black sheep! He had no pride!

Officially, Caroline Clement, now eleven, was living again with her parents and brother. But James, Martha, and James Junior were strangers to her, so she often rejoined Mazo at the Lundys. There Caroline could forget about her unhappy father and the cold Clements.

Mazo de la Roche at about eighteen.

3

Young Women

I gazed and gazed. I felt that never again should I be the same.

M azo, thirteen, had moved the year before to Galt, Ontario (today called Cambridge) with her parents. Mazo and Bertie were living with Will in a hotel in Galt. In Galt, Mazo's education continued in another private school. Mazo never did much homework. Her mother was ambitious for her, but she never supervised Mazo's studying. Mazo also took violin lessons, which she loathed.

Mazo began to read the books of the great nineteenth-century novelists, like Charles Dickens, whom her mother was reading. Mazo also read popular adventure novels, like *Allan Quartermain* by Rider Haggard, which was the sort of book her father most enjoyed. Her father was not a lowbrow though, for he urged her to read the great French author, Balzac. During the evenings in their quarters in the hotel, Mazo and her parents took turns entertaining each other by reciting poetry and reading plays. Bertie might recite a poem like "The Lady of Shalott" by Alfred Lord Tennyson. Will might recite "The Wreck of the Julie Plante" by William Henry Drummond. Mazo might recite "Jabberwocky" by Lewis Carroll. One play the family read aloud together was Shakespeare's *Othello* – until Bertie suddenly decided the play was not suited for someone so young and innocent as Mazo. Mazo and her parents also went to the theatre together, rode around in a buggy together, and walked together.

Yet all this closeness when Will Roche was present did not prevent Bertie and Mazo from feeling gloomy when he was far away. Mazo's father, now a travelling salesman for a clothing company, was going to be away for six weeks. Mazo's mother, Bertie, was ill and unhappy.

Bertie was confined to bed. She had a troublesome bronchial cough that even the dry air of Galt could not cure. She had to use an inhalor and take frequent doses of cough medicine that ruined her appetite. Bertie was very worried about being left with only Mazo to look after her.

Mazo felt a great foreboding. After her father was gone, one thing after another made Mazo brood on the strangeness of life.

One morning Mazo was woken by a roaring sound. It came from the direction of the river, which had been frozen. The ice had broken and the river was rushing through the town. Mazo ran to the window. She could see the broken ice rocking and whirling along.

After breakfast she ran to the grey stone bridge over the river. Below the bridge, she could see uprooted trees in the dark and churning river and a poultry house with the poor hens still inside staring wildly through the broken ice. Then came a slab of ice carrying the body of a sheep and a little lamb standing beside the body.

For a long time, Mazo stood watching, fascinated, asking herself how such things could be. As she stared, the body of a cow passed beneath, and then a living cow.

Finally Mazo tore herself away from the strange scene. She ran back to the hotel to tell her mother about everything she had witnessed.

"Mama," she began. But her mother cut her short. "I can't bear to hear about it!" her mother cried.

Then Mazo noticed that her mother had closed the curtains so she could not see the river.

Mazo and her mother returned to Orillia and the Lundy household, where there was companionship for Mazo and care for Mazo's mother. Mazo and Caroline resumed their sisterhood and their shared, imagined world.

In September 1892, Mazo began to study in the public high school in Orillia. Caroline, who was in poor health, stayed at home until the following year. Caroline's belated attempt to join Mazo in high school did not last long. She finally registered at the age of fifteen in October 1893. Her father died the following year, on August 27, 1894.

No notice of James Clement's death appeared in the Orillia newspaper. His gravestone in the Clement Cemetery in the old Cherry Creek district of Innisfil Township was small and inexpensive.

In 1894, Daniel Lundy accepted a job as supervisor of the woodworking shop at Central Prison in Toronto. He and his family (including Will, Bertie, and Mazo Roche) moved to a two-storey, red-brick house on Dunn Avenue in the Parkdale district in the city's west end. Caroline Clement soon left her mother and brother and joined the Lundy household once again.

Mazo continued with her studies in a public high school, Parkdale Collegiate, and she also took piano lessons at the Metroplitan School of Music. Caroline, who was still suffering from health problems, attended private classes with a few other girls, took banjo lessons, and spent much time at home with Mazo's mother, who was also still ill. Happily, Caroline and Bertie had similar interests, especially sewing. Slowly, as Caroline grew stronger, she joined Mazo more often in all the delightful activities for young women that the city could offer.

The girls walked to Lake Ontario just a few blocks away, rode on the King Street electric tram, sipped sodas at McConkey's at King and Yonge Streets, attended plays at the Princess Theatre, and flirted with neighbourhood boys. They also continued to share their imaginary world, and they still put on plays for family and friends. They worshipped at St. Mark's Anglican Church quite regularly, although they were not particularly religious. They went to the outdoor band concerts at the Home for Incurables.

The Home for Incurables was located across the street from Grandpa Lundy's house in Parkdale. On the evenings of concerts, Mazo and Caroline watched the members of the band pass by with their instruments. They watched twilight deepening to darkness. When they heard the first strains of music in the placid air, they crossed the street and hastened toward the gardens of the Home, watching for the flare of the torches against the blackness of the trees and the glint of the brass of the horns.

Mazo and Caroline submerged themselves in the sauntering crowd. They joined a decorous little group of other young people. When the band broke into "Soldiers of the Queen," their hearts surged with patriotism. Soon Queen Victoria would celebrate her Diamond Jubilee!

Often, as Mazo and Caroline were strolling among the formal flower beds filled with red geraniums and purple asters, they met one of the neighbour boys with his friends. The neighbour boy was named Gordon McGrath. Gordon had a tennis court. Admittedly it was only a lumpy grass court, but Gordon and his friends had fun playing on it. Gordon's widowed mother would sit in the shade of the trees, with a friend or two her own age, watching the young people play.

Although Mazo and Caroline saw Gordon almost every day, it was Gordon's oldest brother that Mazo and Caroline adored. This brother was as remote as a Greek god, and he looked like a god too. He had been in a regiment in Ireland. He played polo. He was tall and athletic. He wore Irish tweeds. The sight of this Adonis always sent Mazo and Caroline scurrying to the windows to rhapsodize over his looks. Once when they were spending an evening playing Crokinole with Gordon and his mother, this brother came in. He showed the girls his stopwatch. Everything he did was perfect! Eventually he married a very rich wife.

∞

The fat pony clopped lazily up the narrow dirt road, stopping now and then to crop a few mouthfuls of long, juicy, green grass. The pony was pulling a small, light cart that easily carried two slender young women.

In the summers of their late adolescence, Mazo and Caroline still vacationed at the south end of Innisfil Township, beside Lake Simcoe. Today, although the young women had set out immediately after breakfast, the late-August sun was already becoming hot by the time they reached the wrought-iron fence of the pioneer cemetery. The heat bugs were buzzing.

The spoiled pony had taken over one hour to travel just four kilometres from Lake Simcoe to the cemetery that Caroline's Grandfather Clement had donated to the old Cherry Creek district more than sixty years earlier.

Mazo, tall and auburn haired, was holding the reins. She halted the pony in the shade of a row of lofty pines, climbed down from the cart, and tied the reins to the fence. Caroline, short and platinum blond, was holding a bouquet of flowers. She slid down from her seat, opened the iron gate, and walked purposefully to a huddled cluster of tombstones at the far end of the graveyard. Like Mazo, Caroline was wearing a simple but pretty cotton dress that reached to her ankles.

Caroline halted first before the small, grey, rectangular gravestone of Mary Jane Clement. She read, "died Oct. 1842, aged 14 years, two months, 23 days." Strange that both Caroline and her father had an older sister named Mary who died young.

Caroline did not stir as Mazo caught up with her and stood silently by her side.

"I remember looking at Mary Elizabeth's grave back when I was six or seven in Grand Forks," said Caroline. "It was a warm spring day, and I stood there wondering when she would wake up. After all, the flowers always woke up in the spring."

"'Wakefield' is a name on one of the tombstones in Newmarket near Grandfather Roche's stone," mused Mazo.

Caroline walked slowly toward the grave of her father's parents. Their stone was by far the tallest in the family plot. It was an obelisk. It was white, while the other, humbler tombstones were grey.

"Grandfather Clement was very domineering from what everyone says," murmured Caroline. "He was a big man with a bushy white beard."

"Lewis James Clement ruled over his wife and ten children like a biblical patriarch in the wilderness," said Mazo. "Innisfil Township was truly wilderness when your grandparents came here. As everyone says, they built the first frame house."

"Grandmother Clement died at '49 years, eight months, 1857,' said Caroline. "Probably worn out from having so many children. Of course Grandfather Clement lived a good long life. He was seventy-five when he died in 1873. Five years before I was born."

Caroline moved toward a small grey grave.

James Clement... Caroline read silently.

"Father's tombstone isn't much bigger than Mary Jane's," said Caroline in a tight voice. "Yet he lived to be sixty-four years old, married, had children, and... did things."

Caroline began to cry. Mazo cried in sympathy.

When the cousins returned to the cart in the shade, they sat for a while without speaking. While Caroline recovered her poise, Mazo looked at the magnificent view from this fragment of what had once been a vast estate owned by Caroline's Grandfather Clement. He had truly been the squire of the district! Why each of his eight surviving children had received at least forty hectares of land – or the equivalent in cash.

Across the road was a wooded ravine: the land sloped downward toward Cherry Creek and then rose to the Willson farm where Hiram and Caroline Willson had homesteaded. Mazo wondered whether Caroline's parents, Martha Willson and James Clement, had met in the ravine for secret trysts when they were young lovers. She couldn't imagine Aunt Martha and Uncle James as young lovers! Aunt Martha was over sixty! Her hair was grey!

Grandma Lundy had been raised on that farm from the age of nine. Caroline had been born on it. The farm was called "The Maples." Cattle and horses grazed in its green meadows lined by stately, leafy trees.

Beyond the Willsons' forty hectares, the shimmering land rose gradually toward the horizon, about three kilometres away. On that horizon Mazo could make out the steeple of the little red-brick Anglican church where Hiram and Caroline Willson were buried: Caroline's maternal grandparents and Mazo's great-grandparents. The church, St. Peter's, had been built in the 1850s, but the pioneers had arrived much earlier. The Clements had come in 1829, the Willsons about ten years later.

Caroline's only inheritance would be her share of twenty hectares of land adjacent to St. Peter's. The land had once been owned by Grandfather Clement, of course. Caroline and her brother would sell the land as soon as they could. They needed the money. Grandfather Clement's will said they could not receive the land until the youngest child, Caroline, turned twenty-one. Another two years to wait.

Mazo could see the narrow old Yonge Street road rising northward up the hill to St. Peter's. In a few moments, the pony would clop up the road past the Willson homestead, turn east, and go back towards Lake Simcoe to Aunt Mary's house. This Mary was Mary Catherine, born Willson, now Mrs. Richard Rogerson.

Mazo could just make out a corner of Uncle Richard's forty hectares. Caroline's widowed mother, Martha, boarded with Aunt Mary now. At the age of seventeen, the beautiful, high-spirited Martha Willson had married the eldest son of the richest man in the neighbourhood of Cherry Creek: James Clement, son of Lewis James Clement. But Martha's life with James Clement had not been easy.

Today Mazo and Caroline were to have dinner with the whole family at Aunt Mary's house. Then they would travel back to Toronto by train.

"We must go now," said Caroline finally. "I'll be all right."

∞

What enormous dinners most of the family ate! No matter whose house it was. Rogersons, Willsons, Clements, Lundys, Roches, Bryans – they were all the same. Year in and year out. Everyone sat around the table talking, squabbling, and eating.

The table was always set with heavy plates and vegetable dishes, squat cruets and large English cutlery. A huge roast of beef, thick gravy, mounds of mashed potatoes and turnips. Strawberry shortcakes, raspberry tarts, pumpkin pies... Everything washed down with endless cups of hot, English-style tea with cream and sugar.

Heavy furniture in the dining room. A dark, polished sideboard. Inside shutters and long curtains of yellow velour, caught back by cable-like cords with tassels at the end. Family portraits in oil, heavily framed...

Today Grandpa Lundy was in a particularly jovial mood. He and Uncle Bryan had gone to the circus together! Grandmother Roche's older brother, Abraham Bryan, was a fast friend of Grandpa Lundy. A childless widower, Uncle Bryan officially lived in Whitby, but he often visited the Danford Roche home in Newmarket and the Daniel Lundy home in Parkdale.

"As you know, Louise, I have not been to a circus in many years, and I care nothing for them, but the old gentleman was anxious to go, and I didn't see how I could get out of accompanying him," said Grandpa Lundy, surveying his full plate.

"Not so, Louise! I've given up circuses and all that sort of thing. I don't take any interest in them," Uncle Bryan objected. "But Daniel would have been terribly disappointed if he didn't see this circus, and I promised to go with him."

Everyone at the table laughed.

"What a pair!" said Grandma Lundy with a smile and a shake of the head as she poured the strong, blackish-brown, scalding-hot tea.

Mazo and Caroline were also in a good mood today. After supper, while the older people played cards in the sitting room and the girls washed and dried the dishes, they kept giggling helplessly. They were planning to punish Gordon for confessing to them that he longed to meet an American girl named Lilly Stacy who had recently moved into the neighbourhood.

Still giggling, Mazo and Caroline got ready for Gordon's regular evening visit.

Mazo put on a new sailor hat that Gordon had never seen. She put the hat on her head at a jaunty angle and then added a veil – something else Gordon had never seen her wear.

When the girls saw Gordon approaching, Mazo sat in a dim corner of the porch where the flowers and vines from a window box filled the air with their scent. She struck the pose of a well-travelled woman of the world.

As Gordon entered the porch, Caroline introduced him to the strange woman.

"Lillian, I should like you to meet our friend, Mr. McGrath," said Caroline. "Gordon, meet Miss Stacy."

The pretend Miss Stacy languidly gave Gordon a limp hand to shake. Gordon seated himself on the porch steps and politely conversed with Miss Stacy, who spoke with a refined American accent. Gordon gave Miss Stacy admiring looks that he had never given Mazo.

The quiet of the street, the scent of flowers, and the moonlight glimmering through the leaves were all very romantic. The trouble was that Mazo and Caroline dared not look at each other in case they began laughing.

After a decent interval, Miss Stacy said she must be going. Gordon at once offered to escort her home.

"I've been wanting so much to meet you, Mr. McGrath," Miss Stacy cooed when she had Gordon to herself.

"I feel just the same about you," Gordon sighed.

"I hope you're not disappointed in me," Miss Stacy twittered.

"Oh no," Gordon protested. "I think you're wonderful."

Never had Gordon said anything like this to Mazo!

"You're so different from any of the men I meet abroad," murmured Miss Stacy.

Gordon bent to peer beneath the brim of Miss Stacy's hat. He met the malicious glitter in Mazo's eyes. Mazo burst out laughing. Caroline was laughing so hard that she had to support herself against a pillar of the porch. Gordon wheeled away and strode home.

The next day Gordon left for the Royal Military College without saying goodbye.

Mazo de la Roche in her early thirties with her father.

4

Breakdown

I have little patience with writers who declare that all their works are composed in an agony of spirit.

At noon on a hot July day, Mazo went with her father to look at Grandpa Lundy in his coffin in the back parlour. All the blinds were closed, so it was like a cool dark night in the house. Still, Mazo could see that there was nothing to be afraid of. Grandpa's face was white as marble, but he was not suffering. Actually, he seemed about to smile.

"Poor Grandpa," said Mazo's father as he stood looking down into the coffin. Tears ran down his cheeks.

∽

For six years, until 1900, Mazo and Caroline had enjoyed a well-balanced youth while they stayed in the Lundy household in Toronto. They had finished growing up. After the death of Grandfather Lundy in his Toronto home and his burial in the old Newmarket cemetery, the extended family slowly dispersed, for Will Roche was not a patriarchal man who could gather weaker beings around him and give them shelter and leadership for long periods.

Oh, at first they stayed together. Will Roche promptly relocated the whole family from out-of-the-way Parkdale to central, fashionable, and dignified Jarvis Street, where important families like the Masseys lived. But soon Will was on the move again, changing jobs and residences frequently. Grandma Lundy sought more permanent quarters with her daughter Eva, now Mrs. James Smith, and son Walter, now an eligible bachelor and a fledgling dentist. Bertie, Mazo, and Caroline followed Will to a long list of addresses in Toronto and vicinity that included 54 Wellington Street, Toronto; Richmond Hill P.O.; and 435 Indian Road, Port Credit.

The Port Credit address, twenty kilometres east of Toronto, was the home of G.A. Reid, a visual artist and a teacher at the Ontario School of Art in Toronto. The Roches stayed in Reid's house several times while Reid was absent. While Caroline remained at home with Bertie, and became absorbed in domestic activities, Mazo attended classes at the School of Art and the University of Toronto.

Mazo was dreaming about going to Paris and becoming a book illustrator. Then suddenly she changed dreams. She thought she might like to become a book writer.

∞

Mazo wanted to write a story and send it to a magazine. She had to do this in secret, so that if she were not successful, no one would know. Of course if she were successful, the family would have a lovely surprise.

Mazo's story would be about French Canadians in the mythical village of St. Loo. She was French, wasn't she? Anyway, her Roche ancestors had been French many generations before, as had Caroline's Clement ancestors. And Will Roche quite often went on business to Montreal, Quebec.

Now, thought Mazo, *how do you write a story?*

You have to be in excruciating agony. Isn't that how it goes? Half starved and living in a freezing cold attic.

Well, I'm not in such dire circumstances. And I just have a few hours to myself. Unfortunately, I will have to write without starving or freezing.

Perhaps excruciating excitement will do. When writers close their eyes, they see shimmering visions of the truth. Don't they?

Luckily nobody was home.

Mazo lay on the sofa in the living room. She tensed her body until it was rigid. She watched the pictures that passed through her mind. She rose from the sofa, went over to her paper and pencil, and wrote.

Then she stretched herself on the sofa again. She tensed her body again. She watched the pictures in her mind again. And again she got up and wrote.

Mazo wrote her story in pencil. Then she copied it out carefully in pen and ink. She had no idea that it should be typed. Finally she put it in a big envelope and sent it to to a magazine called *Munsey's*.

For weeks she was the first person to reach the front door when the postman delivered the mail. Then finally came a small envelope from *Munsey's*. Enclosed was a cheque for fifty dollars. Her story had been accepted for publication!

Mazo finally revealed to her family what she had done. She took Caroline with her when she went to spend the money on a gift for Bertie. They chose an ornate lamp.

Mazo began to write another story. This time she did not keep her activity secret.

∞

Many years later, when Mazo was an established writer, the pretended agony in which she had written her early stories seemed funny. But the real agony she had suffered as a young woman never seemed funny.

One day Mazo felt she had written an especially good story. This feeling was reinforced when Caroline and Bertie read the story and agreed with her. Mazo, full of confidence, mailed the story to *Munsey's*.

She waited and waited. More weeks passed than usual. *Did I forget to put postage on the envelope?* Mazo wondered. *Did the envelope get lost in the mail?*

Mazo could think about nothing but the missing manuscript. Sometimes the pavement and floors beneath her seemed to slope away as though into an abyss.

When Mazo went alone to see the medieval morality play, *Everyman*, she suffered the same strange sensation again. Again there was the abyss. She had been raised Protestant, but suddenly she went to a Catholic church – Saint Michael's Cathedral in Toronto – and knelt at all the stations of the cross. She seemed to be hoping for a miracle, but no miracle happened.

When Mazo returned home, she told her mother and Grandma Lundy what she had done. Grandma Lundy, still a staunch Methodist, glared at her scornfully.

Feeling exhausted, Mazo went upstairs and sat down on her bed. She was trembling all over. Her symptoms did not abate, so her family called the doctor. Mazo hated this doctor and could not talk to him. She felt he was jeering at her. Perhaps he was.

Mazo's illness lasted several years, and for most of this time she couldn't write. Indeed, she couldn't do much of anything. She slept poorly at night. She frequently wept. She was extremely depressed. Yet the especially good story she had sent to *Munsey's* had not been lost, and it was eventually published.

Her illness seems to have been psychosomatic: a so-called "mental" illness or "nervous breakdown."

"I'm done for. I shall never be well again," moaned Mazo when an uncle came to her room and asked how she was feeling. "I'm going to die. Like Grandpa died."

Her uncle laughed angrily.

"You couldn't die," he said. "You couldn't. Not even if you *tried*. There's plenty of time for you to develop. You're only beginning. What you need is a different doctor."

၈

Unfortunately a different doctor was not forthcoming. And perhaps no doctor in her own time and place could have helped her anyway. Had Mazo become severely depressed today, of course, most doctors would have prescribed a drug and arranged for her to receive therapy from a medical professional like a psychiatrist. But in Victorian and Edwardian Canada, no such help was available.

There are many possible reasons for Mazo's emotional collapse. She turned twenty-one in 1900: a time when women's roles were rigidly defined. A woman was expected to become a wife and mother. Period. Yet Mazo longed for a career as an artist – visual or literary – and she knew she could not have both a husband and a career, as one can today. The primitive contraceptives available one hundred years ago were not effective.

What's more, Mazo lived in Canada, a colonial country where careers in the arts were difficult for men and almost impossible for women. Mazo would have been well aware that her chosen path was almost without precedent, and she would have doubted her ability to follow that path successfully. Mazo had no role models because there were no outstanding Canadian-born writers of the female sex when she was young.

Like Mazo, several other Canadian-born, female artists of her generation experienced periods of depression in young adulthood. Painter and writer Emily Carr, born in 1871, had a prolonged nervous breakdown when she was in her early thirties. Writer Lucy Maud Montgomery, born 1874, suffered from low spirits in her twenties and thirties while she lived with her grandmother. Even writer Gabrielle Roy, born thirty years after Mazo in 1909, was incapacitated for several years by intense melancholy while she was in her late twenties and beginning to write.

Other possible reasons for Mazo's prolonged depression lie within her family. Mazo undoubtedly experienced conflicting feelings about her parents. She loved her father; yet she could see that Will Roche had failed to provide a permanent home and steady income for his dependents. Mazo loved her mother; yet she could see that Bertie (Lundy) Roche had been both physically and emotionally ill, not only unable but also unwilling to fulfil her duties as a wife and mother.

In one of the Jalna novels, an artistic character, Finch Whiteoak, a young pianist and composer, suffers a breakdown. In *Whiteoaks of Jalna* Finch falls into despair after he is ridiculed by his older brothers and sister for his interest in the arts. Only after Finch attempts suicide does his family rein in their persecution of the sensitive boy. Perhaps there are parallels between the fictional Finch and the real Mazo.

Mazo watched the tree outside her window while she rested at the Reids' house. She enjoyed the wild beauty of Georgian Bay while she vacationed beside it by herself. She absorbed the friendliness of Lake Simcoe while she vacationed beside it with her family.

Bertie, who was stronger now than in the past, carried endless trays to Mazo's room. Caroline held Mazo closely when the sleep-deprived woman felt overwhelmed by despair. Then, when Mazo was better, Caroline went for long walks with her and shared with her their ever-evolving, imagined world. Talking with her trusted cousin helped Mazo solve her emotional problems.

By the time Mazo moved to Acton, she was feeling better. In 1905, Will Roche bought an old hotel in Acton, renovated it, and renamed it the "Acton House." He also moved his family into a house on Acton's Main Street.

∞

Mazo, a dark, dashing-looking woman wearing a red coat and leopard-skin furs, strode into the hotel. The evening meal was over, and the busy hours between seven and eleven were just commencing.

She stood still for a moment and took a deep breath. A rich smell of ale and spirits filled the air. A sustained flow of men's voices came from all sides, sometimes ebbing to a low drone, sometimes swelling to a vigorous burst of laughter.

The door of the hotel opened behind her and several men passed by her and entered the bar. The noise increased, rose to a hubbub, then suddenly fell to a murmur accented by low laughs, the clink of glasses, the drawing of corks. The smell of dyes, the smell of the tannery, mingled with the smell of the bar. A blue cloud of tobacco smoke formed before her eyes. It floated in long level shreds that moved quiveringly together till they formed one mass that hung like a magic carpet in the hall.

"I must remember this," said Mazo. Then she hurried into the kitchen to help wash the dinner dishes. The hotel was short-staffed tonight.

For the next four or five years, Mazo and Caroline were often seen out and about Acton in a two-wheeled cart pulled by a Shetland pony. The young women's close association with a hotel, when the temperance movement was strong, did not prevent them from close association with the local aristocracy.

Mazo and Caroline probably met the Beardsmore family, owners of the local tannery, in church. The Beardsmores owned a grand home set in beautiful gardens behind high walls. Here they lived a very English life with nannies, governesses, and pony carts.

Caroline became engaged temporarily to one of the young Beardsmore men, so Mazo had a chance to observe Acton's high life closely.

But Mazo did not take an interest in the top-drawer people only. In Acton, she also observed ordinary working people such as the waitresses who toiled in the hotel dining room and the factory workers who boarded at the hotel for an inexpensive rate.

"There came a great rush at dinner time," wrote Mazo in a short story called "Canadian Ida and English Nell," published in 1911. "Nell was set to fill dishes with cabbage, stewed tomatoes, and potatoes, the three for each order. At first she was much confused between the cook's excited face and Edith's rushing out, calling: 'One on beef, rare! – Two on pork! – Beef, on a side! – Soup and fish for a traveller!'"

5

Screams

The years were long and the future stretched endlessly, it seemed, before us. We made no plans but took for granted that all would come out well.

"I have tried many things, but I know now that I was meant to be a farmer," announced Will Roche one day to his family. "I believe there is a great future in farming."

In 1911 Mazo was thirty-two and her father was almost twice that age. Yet Will Roche had never been sick a day in his life. Strong and healthy, tall and handsome, Will was an optimist. Finally he had found his true vocation. Or so he thought.

Bertie, Mazo, and Caroline greeted Will's announcement with delighted approval. The three

Benares Historic House and Bianca de la Roche.

Caroline Clement at about age thirty-three with horse in Bronte.

women had enjoyed their lakeside vacations in the farming country of Innisfil Township during the summers, and now they looked forward to being close to nature all year round. Furthermore, the three women thought that Will's being a gentleman farmer would be much more prestigious than his being a hotel keeper. Oh my goodness! All those drunkards at the hotel bar! It was very difficult indeed to run a respectable establishment.

Eagerly Mazo and Caroline joined Will in perusing advertisements for farms and going off to inspect the most promising properties. (Bertie stayed home. She trusted their judgment.) Soon they found the perfect farm about forty kilometres west of Toronto near the fishing village of Bronte on the shore of Lake Ontario.

Lake Ontario was not a "friendly" lake like Lake Simcoe. So Mazo remarked. It was "a great stretch of water – impersonal as a sea." The huge lake was only about thirty metres from the front door of the house. Certainly the farm was picturesque.

There was not only a lake at the front but also a woods at the back. In the spring the woods would be filled with trilliums and violets. How lovely! There was also an old, wind-bent tree on the highest point of the bluff. How romantic! And there were almost thirty hectares of land. How enormous! There were fields for crops and pasturage. There were two fine orchards, one of apples and one of cherries. There were crops of all the small fruits ripening nicely.

Halton County, where Bronte was located, was a better growing area than York County, where

Newmarket was located, or Simcoe County, where Innisfil Township was located. Halton County was within the eastern limits of Ontario's Niagara fruit belt: one of the most moderate climates in Canada.

Why, Burlington, Bronte, and Oakville were renowned for their strawberries! And the farm had hectares of strawberries. An arrangement was already in place for First Nations people from nearby Brantford to spend the summer picking the crops. Wooden shacks were ready for them in the fields. The place was a paradise! Here Will Roche and his family would be happy!

On their first morning at the farm, Will appeared at breakfast in corduroy breeches, leather leggings, and an Irish tweed jacket. He looked magnificent. Bertie, Mazo, and Caroline agreed that he had created the proper atmosphere. Will appointed himself in charge of breeding pedigreed stock and enlarging the fruit-growing fields. Bertie decided she would raise turkeys. Mazo opted for Leghorn hens. Caroline chose pigs.

The family would not, however, dirty their hands excessively or droop from fatigue. A manager, cook, and farm labourers would do the hard work; meanwhile, the owners would remain genteel. Will would occasionally float on his back in the lake and read an adventure novel. (His neighbours, the Cudmores, dubbed him "W.R. Book.") Will would also absent himself from the farm frequently to bring in extra money by working as a travelling salesman. Bertie and Caroline would have time to read books too, and sew pretty dresses. Mazo would write.

༻

During the first year on the farm, Mazo wrote the outstanding short story titled "Canadian Ida and English Nell." This story, about the working-class British immigrants who laboured at that time in the hotels and factories of southern Ontario, was different from anything she had written before.

"Canadian Ida and English Nell" was a warmly empathetic and carefully observed portrait that revealed Mazo's gift for dramatic situations and witty dialogue. Mazo had witnessed the events on which the story was based while helping in the kitchen and dining room of the hotel in Acton. Clearly, during the past ten years of moving here and there with her parents and Caroline, Mazo had developed from an escapist to a realist. From within the protective but restrictive confines of her family, Mazo could observe life carefully.

Her first stories, written about 1900, had been about an imaginary Quebec that she had never visited. This new story was about a recognizable Ontario that she knew well. Eventually, many years later, the story would form the basis of the novel *Delight*.

The story was published in a Canadian magazine called the *Metropolitan* in June 1911. Already Mazo was signing her work, *de la Roche*, although her father went by plain *Roche*.

༻

Before long during that first year in Bronte, the farm was teeming with life, and the dark figures of the First

Nations people were bent over the strawberry crop. In the evenings the sound of a fiddle wafted from the crowded shacks.

Then, when the strawberry season was at its height, a wild storm whirled from the lake and blew the dust and dirt before it in a cloud that covered all the red strawberries in a coat of grey and left their leaves withered and dry. Luckily there were still the raspberries, cherries, blackberries, Lawton berries, and apples. But the bad luck with the strawberries left the amateur farmers subdued, for the strawberries were one of the most profitable crops.

More misfortune was to come.

There was the high-priced pedigreed cow that had just calved, and was given a bucketful of ice-cold water from the stream. She lay in the stableyard, a great black and white mound, dying. There was the bay gelding, Mike, turned to pasture in a field where the barbed-wire fencing was hanging loose. He cut an artery in his breast...

There was the litter of lusty young pigs, overfed till they became paralyzed and died.

There were the turkey poults drowned in their run when the creek flooded. This same flood overran the stables as well as the poultry house.

But the greatest grief was the loss of Johnny, the bright chestnut horse that Will Roche had given to Caroline and Mazo. A stable boy let him out into deep snow for exercise after a week of inactivity. Johnny, full of joy in the sudden freedom, flung himself in a snowdrift to roll. He rolled. He whinnied in distress, for he could not rise. He had ruptured himself.

As well as these disasters and others with produce, livestock, and pets, one family member after another died in quick succession. Mazo's paternal grandmother, Sarah Roche, died in 1911, as did Caroline's mother, Martha Clement. Mazo's maternal grandmother, Louise Lundy, died in 1913, as did Uncle George Lundy, who was only fifty years old. (Uncle George had sired a son in 1896, when Mazo was seventeen, so she was no longer the only grandchild.)

On the midwinter day in 1913 when Mazo learned that Grandma Lundy was dying, she went outside at bedtime, looked up at the stars, and childishly said aloud: "I have a grandma! I will not let her die!"

That night there was a storm. The sounds of the storm seemed to express Mazo's intense emotions. As she herself explained: "The lake gathered itself together and hurled its strength against the shore. But its thunder could not drown the shrieking of the wind. At times it seemed that a great army was marching down the road... It seemed that the lake was pounding on our very door." Mazo got little sleep in the "savage howling." In the morning there was "brilliant calm" and "icy stillness." Later that day, Grandma Lundy died.

Grandma Lundy's death left the biggest blank in their lives. Never again was Christmas the same. The spirit of the day was so bound up in her.

Of course the sad losses were scattered between happy intervals. The orchards bloomed lavishly, the berries ripened, and the apples filled the shed to the roof. Mazo raised her chickens and wrote. She also entertained two suitors: a Frenchman named Pierre and a Scotsman named Alistair.

Pierre – Fritz Pierre Mansbendel – was especially important to Mazo. He was an engineer from the Alsace region of France. She had met him in Toronto, where she and Caroline went occasionally to see plays and concerts, and he courted her intensely. Ultimately, however, Mazo chose a career over a husband, and Pierre chose a housekeeper over a soulmate. He married his landlady: Mazo's widowed Aunt Eva, who was almost twenty years his senior. The couple moved to New York City. Mazo went back to her writing.

∞

Despite their problems, Mazo, her parents, and Caroline strolled in the evenings through the gorgeous countryside, and talked of all they would do when times were better. Although their financial situation grew steadily worse, they never talked gloomily, for Mazo's parents never gave up hope that conditions would improve. Then one day Mazo realized that the family was refusing to face a loss that was about to destroy their world utterly.

On the first day of autumn 1914, she happened to catch sight of her parents walking through the orchard together. Unseen by them, she observed them closely. Her father was gaunt. His coat was hanging loosely on his broad shoulders. His dark eyes seemed huge and hollow. He was leaning for support on his much shorter wife, Bertie, who was still not strong. Mazo had known her father was ill, but suddenly she realized he was going to die very soon. And he would leave his wife and daughters destitute because he did not actually own the farm itself, only the farm's stock and implements. And there were debts to pay.

Before her parents could see her, Mazo rushed down the shale bluff to the lakeshore. The enormous grey waves roared and hissed on the stony shore. Mazo stood on the stones and stared through dark eyes at the heaving freshwater sea. She screamed. She screamed again. And again. And again. At first she did not realize she was screaming, for she did not hear the sound. No one heard her terrible hoarse cries, which were lost in the thunder of the relentless waves. She did not return to the house until she was fully composed.

Those four years on the Bronte farm had been a slow turning point for Mazo. As her beloved father became weaker financially and physically, Mazo became stronger professionally and emotionally. As Mazo faced the mirror of her grim future on the shore of Lake Ontario in 1914, she knew that her poems and stories brought in little money. She also knew that Caroline, who had worked like a slave on the farm, had few financial resources – just the three hundred dollars she had received when she and her brother sold the land left them by their Grandfather Clement. Mazo knew too that the remaining members of her extended family could offer little or no financial assistance.

Where would they go? What would they do? Who would help them? Mazo was a fearful person. After all, she had suffered a serious nervous breakdown while in her early twenties. Yet now, in her mid-thirties, in a seemingly hopeless situation, Mazo did not allow herself to retreat into fear.

Soon help arrived in the form of a dog.

"As you know," said Will one day in the late fall of 1914, "nothing would please me quite so much for a Christmas present as a puppy. It would be fun for me to train it. It would amuse me when time is heavy on my hands. And I know just where a Scotty could be bought, at a quite reasonable price. It's from champion stock too."

∽

Under the grey sky of winter, the house faced the grey waters of the lake into which slow snowflakes fell and disappeared. Under the white covering of snow, the land slept. To Mazo the sleep seemed not a rest after fruitfulness, not a wait for the glad renewal of spring, but a chill trance of disdain for those whom the land had defeated.

Mazo tried to force herself to be cheerful for Christmas. She looked at the holly wreath on the door and the boughs of balsam above the pictures and the square, small-paned windows. She breathed in the resinous smell of the boughs, the indescribable smell of a pine knot burning.

Mazo, Caroline, and Mazo's parents were sitting around the fire in the parlour when someone knocked on the back door. Mazo went to see who it was. The hired man had finally arrived from the train station with the Scotty Mazo had ordered for her father.

Caroline, Will, and Bertie joined Mazo in the kitchen. The hired man put the small crate in the middle of the kitchen floor, and everyone crowded around. Two glowing black, almond-shaped eyes looked up between the slats at the huge people. The hired man removed one of the slats, put his hand into the crate, lifted out the tiny puppy, and set her on her feet. Unafraid, she wobbled on uncertain puppy legs toward the people. This was Bunty.

Bunty, the black, female Scotty-pup, was a pleasure to Will Roche and his family that last winter on the Bronte farm. She romped with Jock, the collie, and affronted the dignity of Christopher, the cat. Always she could make Will smile. When he sat by the window and stared out at the cold grey lake, Bunty would come and paw Will's leg and he would bend down to pat her or lift her to his knee.

The family played cards during the long evenings of that long winter: Will and Bertie against Caroline and Mazo. Then Will found the games too tiring. Then spring came, and they sold the farm stock and implements for barely enough to pay Will's debts. They were poor. They moved to rented accommodation nearby: half of a house owned by the elderly daughters of a deceased naval officer. Then summer came, and in July Will died.

Strangely, Mazo found she could leash the wild feelings that had almost overwhelmed her that day of the hysterical outcries on the stony shore. Of course she was badly shaken by this sad event. She suffered neuralgic pains in her head, and she felt very tired, so she had to rest more than usual and take relaxing walks in the fresh air. But somehow she carried on. While Caroline and her mother sewed black mourning clothes in Bertie's shadowed room, Mazo slipped into the room where her father had recently died, sat down in his chair, and began to write a humorous story about three mischievous boys.

Sometimes she actually found herself smiling at what she had written. Then the memories of what had taken place in the room would overwhelm her and she would begin to cry. But then she would regain control of herself and pick up her pencil again. While Mazo wrote, or tried to write, Bunty lay at her feet. When Mazo went outside, Bunty led the way.

Soon the practical Caroline had secured a job as a clerk in the provincial parliament buildings in Toronto. Mazo and Bertie joined Caroline in the city, and the three rented an inexpensive house there. With Caroline's small but steady salary, Mazo's occasional sales of stories, and Bunty's example of courageousness, the women somehow managed without Will.

6

"We Two" Against the World

And so our new life began.

"JOAN OF THE BARNYARD – A YOUNG POET-
ESS WHO LOVES CHICKENS," was the title of
an article about Mazo in the Toronto *Star Weekly* of
February 7, 1914. The article featured a picture of
Mazo looking very silly in traditional dairy-maid pose
amidst her Leghorn hens on the farm in Bronte. It
mentioned vaguely that Mazo's writing had appeared in
"American journals." It concluded with one of her
poems.

Evidently the author of the article, Amelia Beers
Garvin, felt that Mazo was a writer to watch, even
though Mazo had not yet written anything longer than

Mazo de la Roche in her late thirties or early forties
with Bunty and Hamish at Lake Simcoe.

a short story. Mrs. Garvin, the literary editor of the Toronto *Mail and Empire*, was also the author of several books. Mrs. Garvin was about the same age as Mazo, but she had accomplished more. Of course Mrs. Garvin had the advantage of wealth and connections: she was a Warnock from Galt, and the Warnocks were related to the Masseys of Toronto.

When Mazo and Bertie joined Caroline in Toronto in the fall of 1915, Mazo continued to write humorous stories about three mischievous boys. She also joined several literary clubs, renewed old acquaintances, and made new friends, including Amelia Beers Garvin. Mazo's continuing creative activity was made possible by Caroline's unfailing emotional and financial support.

Caroline faced those difficult days with a gallant resolution that Mazo was not then experienced enough to appreciate. Mazo just assumed Caroline would support her.

Caroline not only supplied the bread and butter on their plates and the roof over their heads. She also supplied leadership.

"Mazo must go on with her writing," said Caroline. "But we are in very straitened circumstances, and we must change our mode of living drastically. Everything must go. We must economize."

Between 1915 and 1920, the three women remained together. They moved from a duplex on Birchall Avenue in Bronte to a little house on Huron Street in Toronto, then to Collier Street, then to Walker Avenue, then to a different house on Collier, then to a different house on Walker. These were all rented accommodations within walking distance of

Caroline's job. During the summers, as always, they holidayed beside Lake Simcoe. Mazo and Bertie spent the whole summer there; Caroline visited them on weekends and during her two-week annual vacation.

Caroline was doing well. In 1917, she became a statistician in the Fire Marshall's office of the Ontario government. Her salary was raised to six hundred dollars per year. Even when she was haunted by her unhappy past, Caroline kept on working and improving her job status.

In 1919 and 1920, Caroline's older brother was bad news. Literally. "SERIOUS CHARGE HAS BEEN LAID," announced the headline in the *Brantford Expositor* on May 6, 1919. Caroline did not normally read the Brantford paper, but she heard about the article from her family. Her brother had been accused of accepting money for helping someone avoid military service during the First World War.

"HONORABLE ACQUITTAL FOR J.H. CLEMENT," was the headline on May 15, 1919. The judge had acquitted Caroline's brother of this charge, but he had done so before the accuser's lawyer could reach the court! The *Expositor* article about her brother's acquittal ended with a quotation from the accuser's lawyer. "There has been a gross violation of justice," the lawyer declared. "The last has not been heard of it, as I shall institute civil proceedings against Clement to recover $700."

Had Caroline's brother taken a bribe or hadn't he? If he had, he must have been very cynical about his family's distinguished record of military service.

"To the Grave: JAMES HARVEY CLEMENT," read the headline in the *Brantford Expositor* of January 3, 1920. Now Caroline's brother was dead!

On the surface all had seemed well with Caroline's brother, who went by "Harvey." He had married an Orillia girl, moved to Brantford, fathered several children, and risen to the position of foreman of the Verity Plow Company. He had even been elected an alderman for the city of Brantford. Then, as if the bribery charge were not enough, suddenly, on December 31, 1919, he dropped dead at the age of forty-six while on business related to his role as alderman.

Harvey's mysterious death made several more headlines in the Brantford newspaper because an inquest was held. The coroner at the inquest concluded that Harvey had died of heart failure due to an overdose of alcohol. Harvey had drunk too much bootleg whisky from a bottle he was carrying with him. There had been nothing wrong with the whisky; Harvey had just drunk far too much of it.

The coroner also concluded that Harvey had been a chronic alcoholic. This in a period of prohibition!

Why was Harvey drinking so heavily? Had he inherited a tendency toward alcoholism? Did he have marital problems? Did he feel guilty about accepting a bribe?

Poor Caroline! She could not help wondering what had gone wrong with Harvey. After all, most of Harvey's male first cousins were doing very well. They included not only a druggist, an agriculturalist, engineers, lawyers, and aldermen, but also judges and a business magnate. One first cousin, Stephen Clement Junior, who lived in Brandon, Manitoba, had been

mayor of Brandon and a member of the Manitoba leg-
islature, as well as a judge and alderman. Another first-
cousin, Reggie MacMillan, who was Chief Forester of
British Columbia, had recently incorporated a company to sell B.C. lumber products to foreign markets.
Meanwhile, Caroline's brother had tried to keep up
with his successful cousins, but he had been as much a
failure as his father. Poor Harvey!

While Caroline was still mourning her brother,
Mazo's mother died of pneumonia during a flu epi-
demic in the winter of 1920. Mazo and Caroline buried
Bertie beside Will in the old Newmarket cemetery.
They spent their first summer vacation without Bertie
in the same cottage on Lake Simcoe where one year
earlier Bertie had read aloud to them from a copy of
Don Quixote by Miguel de Cervantes. The book had
belonged to Grandfather Roche. They spent their first
Christmas without Bertie at the Toronto home of
Amelia Beers Garvin.

The last living members of both women's immediate families were gone. Now it was "we two" against
the world. In the months following her mother's death,
Mazo began to work on her first novel and several
plays. She also finished writing the series of stories that
would be included in her first published book,
Explorers of the Dawn.

∞

The New York firm Alfred A. Knopf published
Explorers of the Dawn. In 1922 *Explorers of the Dawn*
was on bestseller lists in the United States.

Christopher Morley, an important American author and editor, wrote an introduction to *Explorers of the Dawn*. He called the stories "fanciful" as well as "delicate and humorous" and "refreshing and happy." He compared *Explorers of the Dawn* to *Peter Pan in Kensington Gardens* by James Barrie and *The Wind in the Willows* by Kenneth Grahame.

The main characters in the closely interwoven series of stories are three English boys who wear Eton collars, eat bread pudding, and say things like "bully fun." The three are brothers who live in their governess's house because their mother has died and their father is absent on a long business trip. The boys are high spirited and irreverent. To them, every day is a grand adventure, and all adult authority figures are irrelevant bores.

Beneath the merriment and hijinks is unhappiness. The boys' guardian, their governess, is a kind of wicked stepmother who is as stiff, inhuman, and unloving as the frightening stuffed birds in her parlour. In the end, the boys are rescued and restored to their rightful guardian, their father, who promises them ponies and dogs.

Explorers of the Dawn is very English in many ways. Nevertheless, the stories include details from Mazo's own childhood in Canada. For example, in one of the stories each boy is given a long red banana by an Italian named Salvator. Mazo remembered the long red bananas peddled by an Italian fruit vendor named Salvator Polito in Toronto.

Hugh Eayrs, the president of the Canadian branch of the Macmillan publishing company, invited Mazo to come and have tea with him in his office. Mazo was excited because she admired the influential Englishman and because this would be her first visit to a publisher's office.

It was winter. Before she left her house Mazo had to check the coal furnace in the basement to make sure it was working properly. Before going down to the basement, Mazo put on a shabby old grey sweater with a hole in one elbow to protect the pretty dress she was wearing for the big occasion. When she came back upstairs, she forgot to take the sweater off. She put her muskrat coat on top of the sweater and set out.

Hugh Eayrs welcomed Mazo to his office. A typist brought in the tea things and left. Just as Mr. Eayrs was about to help Mazo off with her coat, he was called out of the office and hurried away. Left alone, Mazo decided to remove her coat herself. She was shocked to discover she was still wearing the ugly old sweater.

What to do? Put the coat back on and insist she could not take it off because she was cold? But the office was hot!

Mazo was in a panic. But then she noticed a window was open to the street. Quickly she removed her grey sweater, rolled it up, and threw it out the window.

"What a pretty dress!" Mr. Eayrs exclaimed when he returned to the office.

As she and the publisher had their tea and got acquainted, Mazo could not stop thinking about her sweater lying in the street. She was afraid someone would walk into the office any moment to return it to her.

But Mazo never saw her old grey sweater again.

She did, however, see Hugh Eayrs, who became her publisher. This was the beginning of a very long association between Mazo and Macmillan, which published her next book – a novel.

Caroline Clement in her forties possibly behind St. Peter's
Anglican Church in Innisfil Township at the edge of land
she inherited from her Grandfather Clement.

7

Possession, Thunder, *and* Delight

Looking back over my life, it is borne in on me how much I have walked. Walk – walk – walk – usually with a dog beside me – over city pavements – along country roads.

Mazo was writing a novel. It was her first novel, and it was called *Possession*. The novel started like this: "On an evening in early May, a young man was walking sharply along the country road that passed through the fishing-village of Mistwell, and following the shore of one of those inland seas, oddly called great lakes, led to the town of Brancepeth, seven miles away."

The main character in *Possession* is a young architect named Derek Vale. Vale inherits a farm called "Grimstone" near Mistwell and goes to live there.

Through his weaknesses and mistakes, Vale almost loses his farm and does lose his true love.

Although engaged to Grace Jerrold, the daughter of an upper-class English neighbour, Derek Vale seduces Fawnie, a beautiful young First Nations employee. Vale's union with Fawnie results in a son named Buckskin. Vale marries Fawnie and provides a home for their son, but Fawnie leaves Vale for a First Nations man, and Buckskin dies because of neglect. Although Fawnie eventually returns to him, and Vale remains faithful to Fawnie, Vale is not happy because he loves Grace, not Fawnie.

In writing *Possession*, Mazo was writing fiction, but she was creating this fiction out of elements from her past experiences. Countless details of *Possession* correspond to details of Mazo's real life. For example, the novel's setting, Grimstone in Mistwell, is a relatively exact rendering of the real Roche farm in Bronte.

Published in 1923 by the Macmillan Company, *Possession* was widely praised in Canada and abroad. Reviewers over and over again made it clear that they were hailing a novel that said something about Canada.

One reviewer wrote: "*Possession* is the best Canadian novel I have ever read."

Another reviewer wrote: "There is no other novel about Canadians that has given us as much pleasure as *Possession*."

∞

Mazo soon learned that the success of one novel did not guarantee the success of another. After she finished writing *Possession*, she travelled to Nova Scotia for a month-long stay. From observations she made of life in that province, she wrote her second novel, *The Thunder of New Wings*.

Echoing her descriptions of Derek Vale, Mazo described the main character, Toby Lashbrook, as "self-willed," often "wrong headed," but "keen," and with the "power of seeing his life as a whole." Like Vale, Lashbrook learns farming. Like Vale, Lashbrook is weak and irresponsible. He has a son by his step-mother, Clara, and his relationship with Clara is not good. He fails to keep his family together, and loses most of his material wealth.

Unfortunately, the novel was unsatisfactory. This time, Mazo did not anchor her fiction with carefully observed, deeply felt material from her real-life experiences. Her knowledge of Nova Scotia was too superficial to sustain a fictional work of several hundred pages.

No publisher wanted *The Thunder of New Wings*. Although Mazo had spent a year working on it, she flung the manuscript into a drawer and tried to forget it by taking long walks with Bunty.

∽

While Mazo was in Nova Scotia, Caroline, who was still working full time in the provincial government, spent a weekend in a guest house in Clarkson, a little village that is now part of the sprawling city of Mississauga, twenty-five kilometres west of Toronto, on Lake Ontario. In Clarkson, Caroline met Florence Livesay, a translator and journalist, the wife of J.F.B. Livesay, the head of Canadian Press.

After the two women drank tea together, they took a walk in the woods near the Livesays' house, and Caroline was delighted by the scenery. Immediately Caroline decided that she and Mazo should buy one of the vacant properties adjacent to the Livesays' home and build a small cottage on it.

Mazo and Caroline called their new summer home "Trail Cottage" because it was located on what had once been a First Nations trail to the Credit River. The woods around the cottage were full of trilliums, blood root, columbines, rare fringed gentian, trailing arbutus, and wintergreen. The rafters of the cottage were unadorned – there was no ceiling – and the walls were of unpainted pine. Trail Cottage consisted of a large living room with an alcove for the kitchen, where Mazo did the cooking.

After a long cold winter in Toronto in rented quarters, Mazo and Caroline were happily spending the summer of 1924 in Trail Cottage. Mazo, undaunted by failure, was working on her third novel, *Delight*. This novel would be different from *The Thunder of New Wings*. This novel would not fail. This novel would be set in Mazo's home province.

After she finished her writing for the day, Mazo always took a long walk with Bunty through the woods. Then she tidied up the cottage and began to get supper ready. After she and Caroline had eaten in the evening, Mazo read Caroline what she had written that day. If Caroline approved, the words stayed as they were.

⚭

The setting of *Delight* was Brancepeth. Brancepeth had characteristics of Acton, Ontario, but it was set beside an "inland sea." Since Acton is located thirty-five kilometres north of Lake Ontario, Mazo evidently borrowed the location of Brancepeth from a town on Lake Ontario, like Oakville or Clarkson or Burlington.

When Mazo wrote *Delight* she had not been in Acton for thirteen years, so she mixed details from her present, visible surroundings with details from her remembered, invisible surroundings. Then she spiced the mixture with invented elements that helped make the story more interesting and universal. Her creative process was complex.

In *Delight*, Mazo wrote about a young woman who has inherited only her grandmother's dishes and must work for a living. Delight Mainprize is the illegitimate daughter of an English chorus girl and a Russian ballet dancer. She has been raised by a lower-class grandmother in rural England. Delight has immigrated to Canada to take a job as a waitress at the Duke of York Hotel in Brancepeth.

Delight Mainprize is a potent combination of beautiful Venus and chaste Diana. She is unconscious of her seductive charms and bewildered by the effect she has on people: men love her and scheme to have her, and women hate her and scheme to destroy her. Delight is a good worker at the Duke of York and a virtuous girlfriend to Jimmy Sykes, but through no fault of her own the other women at work become jealous of her, and Jimmy doubts her virtue.

The women force Delight to leave town. She finds work on a farm where, again through no fault of her own, she is half starved and nearly raped. When she returns to town and begins waitressing at another hotel, the other women try to drown her in the lagoon, and the men try to rescue her.

Delight is tested in love, and she proves to be true. Jimmy Sykes, who wins Delight, is likewise true in love. He is also a good student of nature – hence his knowledge of crows and his fondness for the wild lagoon. As well, Jimmy is the fastest runner among the men who race to rescue Delight.

Jimmy and Delight are naive and powerless. Yet they triumph over adversity. Although *Delight* contains realistic details from lives of ordinary working-class people, it also contains romantic elements from fairy tales and myths.

∞

When the distinguished Toronto literary critic, William Arthur Deacon, began to read *Delight* in 1926, he was both excited and shocked by a detail in the following passage: "The men passed into the bar. The noise increased, rising to a hubbub, then suddenly falling to a murmur accented by low laughs, the clink of glasses, the drawing of corks. The smell of dyes, the smell of the tannery, mingled with the smell of the bar. A blue cloud of tobacco smoke formed before Kirke's eyes. It floated in long level shreds that moved quiveringly together till they formed one mass that hung like a magic carpet in the hall."

The detail that stood out for Deacon was, as he put it, "the blueish tobacco smoke that drifted into the hall over the swing-doors of the bar." As Deacon explained, "This phenomenon had to be seen to be believed; and it was a thing almost extinct in Canada."

Deacon rushed to Jean Graham, an acquaintance of Mazo and the editor of the *Canadian Home Journal*.

"Where did Mazo see that?" Deacon asked Graham.

"Her uncle kept a hotel in Newmarket," Graham replied. No doubt Graham's incorrect answer was based on vague information supplied by Mazo.

Such a specific detail as the floating blue tobacco smoke was and is a mark of excellent writing, as Deacon well knew. Yet frequenting bars was not a socially acceptable activity for a well-brought-up woman, as Deacon also knew. Mazo never told anyone in literary circles about her close association years before with the Acton House, even though the experience had provided her with so much valuable raw material.

Her hotel experiences would remain a secret for many decades, until long after her death.

∞

When *Delight* was published in 1926, the Canadian reviews were cool. Yet the novel's reception in other countries was uniformly favourable.

Mazo complained in a letter to a British critic who had reviewed *Delight* enthusiastically: "Your attitude towards it was so sympathetic and unusual, that I cannot resist letting you know of the pleasure it gave me. The book has not been well received in Canada."

Mazo went on to explain that Canadian reviewers had said that *Delight* was tedious, dull, and hedonistic. They also said that the characters were uninspiring.

Luckily Mazo was a strong person now. A weaker person might have given up. Luckily too, the previous year, 1925, Mazo's play, *Low Life*, had won several competitions: one sponsored by the Toronto-based Imperial Order of the Daughters of the Empire, and one sponsored by the Montreal branch of the Canadian Authors Association. These wins helped remind Mazo that all Canadians did not dislike all her work all the time.

Ironically, many decades after the hostility of Canadian reviewers wounded Mazo in 1926, Canadian academics would single out *Delight* for special praise. In fact, many professors would regard *Delight* as Mazo's best book ever – a Canadian classic!

Mazo was dead by then.

8

The Winner

From the very first the characters created themselves. They leaped from my imagination and from memories of my own family.

"What advice would you give to girls who wish to obtain success as a writer?" asked the reporter.

"Seek solitude, read wisely but not too avidly, and concentrate your mental and physical powers on your work," replied Mazo.

Mazo was talking to Norma Philips Muir, a reporter for the Toronto *Star Weekly* who visited her at Trail Cottage in July 1926. The resulting article was titled, "SHE HAS NEVER SEEN A MOVIE."

Mazo de la Roche at Trail Cottage in the 1920s walking Bunty.

Mazo herself was concentrating her powers on her work. She was seeking solitude at Trail Cottage and writing a novel that she had been thinking about for several years. Two characters had come into her mind: a middle-aged man and his older sister. These characters became Renny and Meg Whiteoak. A house had come into her mind. Actually she had been dreaming about a house over and over again.

In the dream, Mazo was walking alone across a wide stretch of sandy beach by the sea. Beyond the beach stretched a sunny moorland and, at its edge, facing the sea, stood a house, with all its doors and windows open. The house looked cheerful and welcoming, and Mazo could see that it was sparsely furnished. One room had nothing in it but a table and a chair or two. There were no curtains, no pictures, and no one was living in the house. Yet the house was not desolate. A most beautiful and comforting radiance emanated from the house – a luminosity. Yet there was nothing ethereal about the house. It was very real and Mazo was terribly eager to go into it – to live there. Yet always, as Mazo reached the doorsill, the house faded and was gone.

The disappointment of the dream became the satisfaction of the story as Mazo wrote more and more about a big, handsome, red-brick house located on an enormous rural property. In the 1850s, Mazo imagined, Captain Philip Whiteoak had bought four hundred hectares of "rich land." This land was "traversed by a deep ravine through which ran a stream lively with speckled trout. Some of the land was cleared, but the greater part presented the virgin grandeur of the primeval forest."

Captain Whiteoak had employed a "small army of men" to "make the semblance of an English park in the forest, and to build a house that should overshadow all others in the county. When completed, decorated, and furnished, it was the wonder of the countryside. It was a square house of dark red brick, and a wide stone porch, a deep basement where the kitchens and servants' quarters were situated, an immense drawing-room, a library…"

Mazo's new novel would be set in the 1920s. As the novel began, Captain Whiteoak would be long dead, but his widow and descendants would have lived in the house he had built for more than seventy years, or three generations. Similarly the Whiteoaks' neighbours, the Vaughans, would have lived in their house on the other side of the ravine for three generations.

Caroline had taken the early morning train from Clarkson to her civil service job in Toronto. In Trail Cottage, Bunty was snoozing and Mazo was seated in the rocking chair in which her Grandmother Roche had soothed her baby sons: Danford, William, and Francis. Beside Mazo on the floor was her dictionary consisting of the two massive old leather-bound volumes compiled by the great Dr. Samuel Johnson several centuries earlier. These heavy, valuable books had belonged to Grandfather Roche.

With a drawing board on her knee, Mazo sat straight and wrote with a pencil. When she could not think of the right word, she rocked. When she did think of the right word, she stopped rocking and wrote it down. When she was not certain of the meaning of a word, she heaved up one of the volumes of the dictionary. Often she became so fascinated by other words that she forgot the one she was searching for.

Still, this fourth novel was going well. It opened with the youngest member of the Whiteoak clan, an eight-year-old rascal named Wakefield, running through a field on a beautiful spring day: "Wakefield Whiteoak ran on and on, faster and faster, till he could run no farther. He did not know why he had suddenly increased his speed. He did not even know why he ran."

Mazo invented details and scenes and even people. She also added things from her immediate surroundings. But in large measure the fictional Whiteoak family was modelled on a combination of the families of Mazo and Caroline.

Grandfather Whiteoak built a handsome red-brick house on his land because Mazo's Great-great-grandfather Lundy had built a handsome, red-brick house on his land. Great-grandfather Whiteoak was killed during the Battle of Waterloo because Caroline's Great-grandfather Clement had been killed during the War of 1812. The grandparents of Renny and Meg Whiteoak pioneered in the wilderness of Canada because the grandparents of Caroline had pioneered in the wilderness of Canada, as had the great-great-grandparents of Mazo.

Many generations of Clements had been officers in the British army, so many generations of Whiteoaks would be officers too. Grandpa Lundy's ancestors were of English origin before they were American, so

Grandfather Whiteoak's ancestors were English. Grandma Lundy had Irish connections, and Grandmother Roche had been born in Ireland, so Gran Whiteoak was Irish.

That summer at Trail Cottage, Mazo lived with the Whiteoaks, completely absorbed by them. To create the Whiteoaks, she wove together present and past, here and there, real and imagined.

At present she was staying beside Lake Ontario, but Mazo often recalled her past vacations beside Lake Simcoe, as well as her earliest years in Newmarket. She had good reason to be nostalgic, for the places and people of her childhood and youth had disappeared almost entirely.

The farm south of Newmarket where Mazo's Grandpa Lundy had been born and raised had been sold out of the family in 1920 while Mazo and Caroline were mourning the deaths of Bertie Roche and James Harvey Clement. Three years later, in 1923, Mazo's Uncle Danford Roche had died, as had the last of Caroline's paternal uncles, Uncle David Clement.

And now Uncle David Clement's widow and children were selling his land, which included the frame house that Grandfather Clement had built almost one century earlier. Uncle David's children did not want to farm.

The last of the Willson sisters, Aunt Mary (Willson) Rogerson, had died in 1924. And now Aunt Mary's only son was selling that land too. He did not want to farm either.

Uncle David Clement and Aunt Mary Rogerson both lay in the pioneer Clement Cemetery now. How well Mazo remembered the view from the gates of that cemetery!

Mazo imagined herself standing at the gates of the Clement Cemetery with her back to the frame house built by Grandfather Clement. She imagined that the old red-brick house of Great-great-grandfather Lundy was behind her back instead. She imagined that the 1828 Lundy house was superimposed on the property that Grandfather Clement had acquired from the Crown in 1828.

Combining the Lundy house and Clement land was a way of expressing the sisterhood that Mazo and Caroline felt and lived, even though they were just cousins. It was a way of saying that Caroline Clement had become a Lundy – almost.

Mazo remembered that in the old days in Cherry Creek, there was Willsons' Hill and Clements' Hill. She imagined that the Willsons were called the Vaughans, and the Clements, blended with the Lundys, were called the Whiteoaks.

Mazo remembered that there was still one last Clement grandson and one last Willson grandson farming in the old Cherry Creek district of Innisfil Township – now called Fennell.

The Clement grandson, Robert Clement, farmed half of Grandfather Clement's original eighty-hectare grant from the Crown. The Willson grandson, Norman Willson, farmed the forty hectares of Grandfather Willson.

These last grandsons – cousins of Mazo and Caroline – were symbols to Mazo of a passing way of life. The other grandchildren were scattered from

Buffalo, New York to Vancouver, British Columbia. They were working as everything from marine engineer to forester.

The fictional characters, Renny Whiteoak and Maurice Vaughan, would also be symbols for a passing way of life. A traditional life. A life that revolved around the seasons of the year. A life that was tied to the land. Land that was handed down from father to son...

The Clements loved horses... Of course Will Roche had loved horses too. And dogs even more than horses...

That clinched it! Renny Whiteoak must be a horse-and-dog man! He must raise thoroughbred horses! And he must own purebred dogs.

Renny would not hunt foxes like the wealthy did. He would be fox-like himself, lodged in his comfortable old home as a fox is lodged in his burrow. Renny would not be rich. He would be hounded by creditors...

Mazo also thought about the place where she and Caroline were now staying and the people who lived there. Trail Cottage, which was little more than a shack, was located near a stately house called Benares. Benares, named after a military station in India, had been built about seventy years earlier by a Captain James Harris. Oddly, Benares reminded Mazo of the lost past of Caroline and herself.

Like the home of Grandfather Clement, Benares was located a few kilometres away from an Anglican church named St. Peter's. Also like the home of Grandfather Clement, Benares was located a few kilometres away from a large lake. Like the home of Great-great-grandfather Lundy (and that of Great-grand-father Clement in Niagara), Benares was of Georgian or Colonial style. Actually, Benares had a similar floor plan to the home of Great-great-grandfather Lundy; it was also made of red brick; and its grounds were very similar in size, shape, and topography!

Mazo decided that, like the real Captain James Harris, the fictional Captain Philip Whiteoak had named his Canadian home after his home in India. Mazo's Great-great-grandfather Bryan *might* have gone to India with the British army. After all, he had been in the Royal Artillery. So why not have Grandfather Philip Whiteoak stationed in India before he emigrated to Canada? It sounded exotic and suggested the vastness of the British Empire in the nineteenth century. What's more, it offered a possibility for a catchy title.

Mazo chose the name "Jalna" from a list of British military stations in India provided by a man in Caroline's government department. "Jalna" was short and looked good when Mazo wrote it out.

∞

In 1925 and 1926, while Mazo was working on the novel she titled *Jalna*, she was not altogether isolated. In both Toronto and Clarkson, Mazo and Caroline had friends whom they visited regularly. In Toronto, Mazo was still a member of several writers' organizations, including the Canadian Authors Association, and by now she was acquainted with well-known writers such as Morley Callaghan, Raymond Knister, and Charles

G.D. Roberts. In Clarkson, there were the Livesays for companionship: not only Fred and Florence but also Dorothy, their precocious older daughter, a poet. Dorothy Livesay, born in 1909, began attending university in Toronto in the fall of 1926. She would go on to become one of Canada's foremost poets.

Mazo finished *Jalna* late in 1926, shortly after she and Caroline moved to a new, upstairs flat at 86 Yorkville Avenue in Toronto, a house owned by Gertrude Pringle, a niece of Ernest Thompson Seton, the famous Canadian author of *Wild Animals I Have Known*. Pringle herself was the author of a book about etiquette.

∞

Mazo ended *Jalna* with a scene featuring the oldest member of the Whiteoak clan, Gran Whiteoak. The old matriarch, Adeline Whiteoak, is celebrating her one-hundredth birthday. Surrounded by her family, she is sitting in a "pool of serene radiance." Over her shoulders is a "black velvet cloak, lined with crimson silk." Her hands, "glittering with rings," are "resting on the top of her gold-headed ebony stick."

Gran Whiteoak is rich and cunning, as well as old. Throughout the novel she has kept her family in suspense as to who will inherit her fortune.

Renny Whiteoak, almost forty and Gran's oldest grandson, is the prime candidate to inherit. He has already inherited the house and grounds from his deceased father, Gran's third and youngest son, Philip Whiteoak Junior. Renny is the manager of the estate and the head of the family. But is Renny worthy of his authoritative position? True, the other candidates all have obvious flaws: Eden is unfeeling and unfaithful, Piers is ignorant and headstrong, Finch is strange and awkward, and Wakefield is selfish and insincere. But Renny is not perfect either. He seems to care more about horses and dogs than people. He has not been tested in love.

In the early chapters of *Jalna*, two of the younger Whiteoak brothers, both in their twenties, suddenly marry. Farmer Piers elopes with lovely Pheasant Vaughan, the girl next door whom he secretly meets in the wooded ravine. But Pheasant is the illegitimate daughter of Maurice Vaughan, who was once engaged to Meg Whiteoak, when he and Meg were young. Meg had called off her marriage to Maurice because of the birth of Pheasant!... Then poet Eden wins the sophisticated Alayne Archer in New York City. But Eden is a cynical scoundrel.

Outraged at Piers's betrayal, Meg, now middle-aged but still angry with Maurice, leaves Jalna in protest. Then Finch, an intense, artistic adolescent, is horrified to discover that Eden is dallying with Pheasant. Finch tells on the adulterers. Piers's marriage to Pheasant is damaged, and Eden's marriage to Alayne is destroyed. Piers forgives Pheasant, and Eden flees. Now Renny can openly express his secret love for Alayne. But will he?

∞

Mazo sent the manuscript of *Jalna* to Macmillan, her usual publisher, and it was accepted. But before the type was set, Mazo heard about an international competition being jointly sponsored by the *Atlantic Monthly* (a magazine) and Little, Brown, and Company (a book publisher), both based in Boston, Massachusetts, U.S.A. The closing date of the competition was February 17, 1927. Macmillan released the manuscript so Mazo could enter the competition.

In Boston, the first reader of Mazo's manuscript was a librarian from the Boston Public Library. She did not like *Jalna*.

"This is the story of a large love-making family in Canada, dominated by the old grandmother," reported the librarian. "The brothers have unseemly affairs with their sisters-in-law, and there is quite a lot about the stable, including the odour. Not recommended."

Jalna became a contender for the prize only after Edward Weeks, a member of the editorial board of the *Atlantic Monthly*, picked up the manuscript because he was intrigued by its title and impressed by its professional typing. He read it and liked it. He passed it to the other readers.

Over the next two months, the field of 1117 entries was narrowed to twelve, then six, and then one unanimous choice.

In the spring of 1927, Mazo received congratulations in the form of telegrams and bouquets from acquaintances, a letter from Prime Minister Mackenzie King, and dinner invitations from important institutions. At the most impressive dinner, the City of Toronto gave Mazo a silver tea service. Mazo thanked the City of Toronto, and called it the city of her birth. (This was a little white lie.) Then Charles G.D. Roberts toasted

Mazo and thanked her for having "proved beyond a doubt that there actually is something called Canadian literature."

At another dinner, the Arts and Letters Club gave Mazo a life-sized portrait of Bunty. (Mazo cherished the portrait for years.)

In the fall of the same year, *Jalna* was advertised in every important newspaper in the United States and Canada. On October 7, the book was published. Within a month, eighty-five thousand copies sold. *Jalna* went on selling extraordinarily well. Mazo, already rich from the prize, rapidly earned a fortune from royalties. Happily, her money troubles were over.

Unhappily, her nervous troubles soon returned. After her 1927 win, Mazo became a public figure. This meant she had to deal with many people very often, something she found difficult.

When her publishers asked for a photo of her, Mazo sent a snapshot taken when she was in hiding in Niagara Falls before the *Jalna* win was announced. Bunty in the foreground and the Spirella Corset factory in the background looked fine, but Mazo in the middle did not look like a winner.

Mazo did not photograph well because she was at ease only in private. "In privacy I can find myself," she explained once, "and the creative impulse in me can move unhampered."

Despite her need for privacy, Mazo kept on accepting invitations to party or to speak. Partying fatigued her because of the smoke-filled rooms and late hours. Public speaking perturbed her because of her nervous disposition.

For days before she had to give a speech, Mazo sank into gloom. At the moment when she had to rise to her feet in front of the audience, her heart pounded painfully. Once she began speaking, she became calm and inevitably she gave a good talk – usually quite funny. But for days afterwards she could not concentrate well enough to write.

She now received many letters to which she must reply. Ambitious writers sent her manuscripts to critique, or they actually brought the manuscripts to her home, and they did not know when to leave. Reporters came from newspapers.

Soon Mazo was sliding into another breakdown.

9

Goodbye Canada!

There followed exciting times for us.

M azo wanted to finish writing the sequel to *Jalna*.
But she could not.

.   Exhaustion and strain were not her only problems.
Grief also prevented her from writing. In June of 1927 the
last of the Roche brothers, Uncle Francis, had died at only
sixty-two. (Uncle Danford had died at seventy-two, and
Mazo was now supporting his widow, Aunty Ida, whom he
had left destitute.) Uncle Francis had become an
extremely successful lawyer. He had married the daughter
of a United States senator. He had run for political office,
twice contesting Toronto seats in Canada's federal
Parliament. Sadly, however, his health had deteriorated.

Caroline Clement in London In 1937.

Then on Boxing Day that year, Bunty died. Mazo and Caroline took her body to Trail Cottage, and John Bird, a local man who was their gardener and woodcutter, dug a grave beneath the snow. The women erected a stone in Bunty's memory, for which Mazo borrowed a line from the great English poet, Lord Byron: "Virtue of man, without his vices."

That winter, Mazo was plagued by acute pains that constantly crawled over her forehead and down the back of her neck. She could hardly write a word.

A doctor recommended that she rest and drink a glass of Scotch whisky and hot water each night before going to bed.

Mazo could not rest. The whisky aggravated her rather than soothing her.

The doctor recommended that she go to the hospital "for electrical treatments."

After each treatment Mazo was worse.

A nurse recommended that Mazo stop the treatments.

She stopped.

Caroline, who had risen to Chief Statistician of the Fire Marshall's office, left her job with the provincial government. Because her salary was not needed now, she could stay home with Mazo and help her. Caroline read aloud to Mazo. She gently massaged Mazo's forehead and neck. She politely dealt with people who made demands on Mazo's time and energy.

Spring came. The pair went for a holiday at a guest house in the Niagara Peninsula where Mazo was unknown. Then, refreshed, they went to Trail Cottage.

One June morning Mazo began to work once again on *Whiteoaks of Jalna*. She had blank paper. She had a new pencil. She had Johnson's *Dictionary*. She had seclusion. Now all she had to do was to put pencil to paper. To write!

She wrote one line. Then her nerves went rigid. She stared at the paper helplessly. One line! Ten words! And she could not write another line.

She was not depressed, she was hopeful. One line was a beginning. Tomorrow she would try again.

The next day she wrote one more line.

The third day she wrote six lines.

The fourth day she wrote half a page.

By the end of the week she had written only one whole page.

"You are getting along very slowly in writing this book," said Caroline. "I am wondering if it would be possible for you to dictate a little of it every morning to me. Even if it were only half a page, it would be something to help you till your nerves are quite well again."

The next morning Mazo placed a blank sheet of paper on the table. Caroline moved a chair to the table. Mazo sat beside Caroline and waited for the words to come. They came, with hesitancy at first, then as fast as Caroline could write. A few hours later the page was covered with writing.

Once again Mazo was absorbed by her characters. Sometimes she was Finch. Sometimes she was old Adeline. Sometimes she agreed with Renny. Sometimes she disagreed.

Whiteoaks of Jalna began to develop more and more rapidly. Mazo and Caroline stayed late at Trail

Cottage. At last, in early October 1928, the novel was completed. The finished manuscript, on which the women's handwriting appeared turn and turn about, was a testament to their perfect harmony.

Caroline was the leader of the pair, yet she was not domineering. Caroline helped Mazo accomplish much more than she could have otherwise. She gave Mazo more confidence in herself. She did this by being exquisitely receptive, like a crystal goblet held beneath a golden tap.

Always Caroline could be a perfect partner in Mazo's creative process, able to set aside her dominant nature and lose herself in Mazo's imaginings. Also, Caroline had a clear critical mind. She could act as an editor for Mazo. Theirs was one of the most remarkable literary partnerships of all time.

∽

The American magazine *Cosmopolitan* wanted to publish *Whiteoaks of Jalna* as a serial. The editor offered Mazo twenty-five thousand dollars, but said that she would have to change the ending.

Mazo wavered.

Caroline looked Mazo firmly in the eyes.

"You are not to attempt it," Caroline said. "It would ruin the story. It would be madness."

"But twenty-five thousand dollars..." moaned Mazo.

"What is twenty-five thousand dollars?" Caroline demanded scornfully. "I won't let you do it."

Whiteoaks of Jalna, its ending unchanged, was serialized in the *Atlantic Monthly*.

∞

When the *Atlantic Monthly* editor read the manuscript of *Whiteoaks of Jalna* he was jubilant. He thought the sequel was superior to the original. He felt Mazo's abilities were increasing. When the editor at the Canadian branch of Macmillan read it, he called it a "stunning performance."

Within two weeks of its publication in book form in 1929, *Whiteoaks of Jalna* was in second place on the national bestseller list in the United States. For Mazo the triumph was personal as well as literary. Her gratitude to Caroline was profound and lasting.

∞

By April 4, 1928, the day Caroline turned fifty, Mazo and Caroline were talking of travelling abroad. At last they could see for themselves places they had only read about and imagined. At last they could get away from the glare of publicity in Toronto and just be themselves. By January 15, 1929, the day Mazo turned fifty, the pair were enjoying the summer-like temperatures of Italy.

Mazo and Caroline had embarked from New York City on the steamship *Vulcania*. Unfortunately, Mazo had to endure more publicity before she found blissful anonymity. Her American publishers, eager to make use of her presence to generate extra sales of *Whiteoaks of Jalna*, arranged an elaborate lunch on board the ship just before it left. Mazo was the guest of honour. The sixty-five invited guests included prominent journalists, representatives of the Literary Guild and the Book of the Month Club, and all the important book buyers in the city. After the lunch, a photographer from the *New York Times* took pictures of Mazo on the deck.

Mazo kept the photograph in which she was wearing a great bunch of violets and looking rather like a movie star. But that night in her stateroom she cast herself on her berth completely exhausted and burst into tears. *Now I know how movie stars feel when they take an overdose of sleeping tablets and end all publicity!* thought Mazo.

Fortunately, the thrill of her first Atlantic crossing soon lifted her spirits. Despite several days of seasickness, Mazo enjoyed the voyage. Mazo and Caroline spent six weeks in Naples and three months in Taormina, and then they took a slow boat to England. After a short stay in London, they moved to Devon, the ancient home of Grandpa Lundy's paternal ancestors. Soon Mazo was writing a book-length biography of Bunty. Her mind turned to those painful days in Bronte.

Mazo felt as though Devon were protecting her. She felt happy and secure. But as she recalled those scenes in Canada, all else faded. Those scenes were her reality.

Writing and remembering brought back the pains in her head and neck, so once again Caroline did the actual writing when Mazo could not put pencil to paper. Mazo just spoke aloud the words that occurred to her. As the months passed, and Mazo and Caroline moved from one rented house to another in Devon, the book progressed. Finally, in October 1929, while the women were living in a splendid old farmhouse called Seckington, *Portrait of a Dog* was finished. The very same day, Mazo began a new novel: *Finch's Fortune*. The new novel would be the third installment of the Jalna series.

∞

Mazo wrote in *Finch's Fortune*: "There they were, crowded into a taxi, making their way through the traffic of the London streets – Finch on one of the drop-seats, almost dislocating his neck in the effort to see out of both windows at once. It was too unreal, seeing the places he had heard of so familiarly all his life. Westminster Bridge, the Houses of Parliament, Trafalgar Square, the lions, Buckingham Palace! They thundered at him like a series of explosions. It was too much. It was overwhelming."

As she wrote these lines, she was using memories from the recent past, when she and Caroline arrived in England. Mazo's trip to London and Devon became Finch's trip to London and Devon, so Finch's trip was like a documentary in some ways. But Mazo was also inventing.

In *Finch's Fortune*, Finch Whiteoak turns twenty-one and receives the enormous inheritance his grandmother has left him. Although Finch generously gives large amounts of money to Piers and Meg, offers money to Renny, and takes his uncles on a longed-for trip to England, the family still criticizes him. Yet Gran seems to have shown wisdom in leaving her money to

Finch. Renny, the head of the household, is showing poor judgment. He is spending all his time in the stables, neglecting his wife Alayne, and refusing to advise Finch on how to invest his money.

Finch joins his uncles on their trip to England and there begins to see his family in better perspective. He also meets a distant cousin with whom he falls in love. But she seems to love someone else – Finch's best friend. Finch suffers his second breakdown. Will he recover?

Finch's Fortune was published in 1931, the year Mazo and Caroline embarked on parenthood.

Mazo and her young adopted children, Esmée and René.

10

Children

Our little family of two suddenly had become four.

While Mazo was writing *Finch's Fortune*, she and Caroline were enjoying themselves. They visited London several times and met fascinating people like Walter Allward, a Canadian sculptor who was working on a memorial for Vimy Ridge, the battle of the First World War in which many thousands of Canadians had been killed or wounded. They also went to see a Canadian actor, Raymond Massey, who had a role in a play at the Savoy theatre. Massey introduced Mazo to other actors who were enthusiastic about the potential of *Jalna* as a play.

Then in 1930 Mazo and Caroline took a four-month trip to North America to visit their old friends, relations, and acquaintances. They returned to England slowly, stopping in the Canary Islands, Casablanca, Algiers, Majorca, Naples, Taormina, Rome, Fiesole, and Paris. By the time they got back to Devon, Mazo had finished *Finch's Fortune*, written several short stories, and begun a non-Jalna novel called *Lark Ascending*.

During these seemingly idyllic years of wandering and scribbling, Mazo and Caroline must have yearned for something more, for suddenly in 1931 they acquired two small children. The girl was about two-and-a-half years old, and the boy was about nine months. Mazo and Caroline named the girl "Esmée Verschoyle de la Roche." They named the boy "René Richmond de la Roche."

Where had the children come from? Whose children were they? Mazo and Caroline gave different information to different people, and some of the "information" was pure fiction. They never even told the children who they were.

Mazo told one person that the children had been left badly off by a dear friend of hers. She told another person that she and Caroline had met the children's parents in Italy, that the father had died six months before the boy's birth, and that the mother had died soon after the birth. Mazo told one person that the children's parents had been killed in a car accident, and she told another that the parents had died of tuberculosis.

Some people speculated that Mazo was the birth mother of the children. Others speculated that Caroline was the birth mother. But, since (like most women of their day) Mazo and Caroline lied about their age, telling people they were younger than they were, no one except close relatives knew that both women were about fifty when the children were born. This fact makes their having given birth to either child very unlikely.

The whole truth has yet to be revealed, but a few more facts are known today. Recently Esmée (now Mrs. Rees) managed to obtain her birth and adoption certificates through a lawyer in England. Her birth certificate shows that Esmée's original given-names were Margaret Elizabeth. It also shows that Esmée was born November 11, 1928 at Snug Cot, Selsea Avenue, Herne Bay. Herne Bay is a small town on the east coast of England in Kent County.

The full name of Esmée's mother was Sybil Andrews Tester. The name of Esmée's father is not given on the documents. The name Norah Andrews Tester appears on an appendix to the birth certificate. Presumably this is Sybil's sister or mother.

A recent online search of public records in the United Kingdom indicates that a person named Sybil Andrews Tester was born about 1906 in Lancaster, Lancashire, England. This Sybil had an older sister named Norah Andrews Tester, born about 1903.

What of the other child that Mazo and Caroline adopted? Who was he? Unfortunately, all that is known is that he was born June 12, 1930 and that Mazo and Caroline always referred to him as Esmée's natural brother. René died in 1984.

Were Esmée and René really brother and sister?

The children's colouring differed. Esmée's eyes were greyish blue, her eyelashes and eyebrows were dark, and her hair was the colour of pale honey. René's eyes were brown and his hair was reddish gold. But the children do look alike in the black-and-white photographs of them taken when they were first adopted. The children's temperaments also differed. Esmée was lively, a little overbearing, and undemonstrative. René was gentle and affectionate. But birth order and different initial environments would help explain the children's having different temperaments. Besides, most siblings do not look or act exactly alike.

Likely the children shared the same mother. Probably they also shared the same father.

∞

In April 1931, Mazo and Caroline took the children to their Devon home, the farmhouse called Seckington. A few months later, the family left that house, which was too small and inconvenient, and moved to The Rectory in Hawkchurch Parish. The Rectory was a picturesque old dwelling with stone-mullioned windows arched like those of a cathedral. On the main floor there was a drawing room, dining room, and study. On the second floor there were three bedrooms, two dressing rooms, two nurseries, the bathroom, and a small room that Caroline used for typing. On the third floor there were bedrooms for the cook and the house parlourmaid.

The nurse – the woman who looked after the children – slept in the nursery. The man who worked as the gardener, chauffeur, and handyman slept in his own cottage.

Mazo and Caroline had begun to live an imitation of upper-class English life.

Mazo was not an acquisitive person, but Caroline wanted to live in a setting that suited their new circumstances. Caroline liked The Rectory. She felt it was a lovely, peaceful spot. While Mazo did her writing, Caroline had a wonderful time going around to the country auctions, buying furniture for the big old house.

Meanwhile the children spent most of their day with the staff. Charles Chant, the gardener/chauffeur/handyman, was a kind person who would seat the children on his shoulders while he marched along the garden paths. One of René's first words was "Cha" for Chant. He called the cook "Coo-coo." Both children shrieked with laughter as their nurse, or "nanny," gave them their baths. They also enjoyed their hour or so after tea time with Mazo and Caroline, when all four danced to records on the gramophone. "The Teddy Bears' Picnic" was a favourite.

∞

Mazo watched from the window of her study at The Rectory. Nurse had put little Esmée and René out on the gravel sweep, where it was dry, to enjoy the morning air. Nurse had provided the children with toys for their amusement before leaving them, but they were not playing. They were content to stare up at the moving clouds and the rooks, blown like flying leaves across the sky.

The children were dressed alike in fawn-coloured woollen suits and caps. Esmée was sitting in the chair. René occupied the perambulator.

"Caw! Caw! Caw!" cried the rooks. The black crow-like birds looked as though they were swimming in the wind. Now they were dipping low toward the dark mass of the ancient yew tree. Now they were rising high above the church tower.

The clock in the tower began to strike heavy, clanging strokes in the heavy air.

The children started as the first loud stroke assailed their sensitive ears. They looked at each other in alarm. But they recovered themselves almost at once and gazed up at the sky. They seemed to think that the strokes came from somewhere in the sky's grey vastness.

Ten of them! It was ten o'clock.

The window of the nursery opened above Mazo's head on the second floor.

Nurse threw two rusks down to the children like manna from the skies.

"Here are your rusks!" called Nurse. "Come Esmée. Take Baby his. There – on the grass – don't you see?"

Esmée rose from her chair and stumped to the strip of grass under the nursery window. She saw the rusks but she was not sure that she would pick them up. From the row of windows just above her head came a pleasant warm smell. In there was the kitchen, but Esmée did not realize that, although once she was inside she was very much at home.

Nurse leaned out of the window, peering down at the children. René leaned over the side of the pram to see the rusks lying on the grass.

"Pick them up at once," ordered Nurse. "And give one to Baby."

Esmée picked up the rusks and, trotting briskly to the pram, presented René with his. They began to crunch them, staring at each other...

Mazo jotted down a description of the scene. With only a few changes, she would include it in a little book about the children titled *Beside a Norman Tower*.

∞

Mazo finished *Lark Ascending* during the first few weeks at The Rectory. This novel, about a lazy painter named Diego Vargas and his hard-working cousin, Josie Froward, was indirectly a satire on Mazo and a tribute to Caroline.

Josie runs a bakery and sells antiques to support Diego and his equally self-centred mother, Fay. Similarly Caroline worked many years in the Ontario government to support Mazo and her mother, Bertie. Josie always finishes Diego's paintings. Similarly Caroline always critiqued Mazo's writing. Josie finally leaves Diego and Fay and marries a good man who appreciates her. Of course Mazo hoped Caroline would never leave her.

Immediately after completing this novel, set in New England and Sicily, Mazo began writing once again about Canada. Now Mazo's imagination returned to the Whiteoaks and took up the story where *Finch's Fortune* had left off.

As *The Master of Jalna* opens, Renny is forty-five years old and living at Jalna with Alayne and their first child, an eighteen-month-old girl named Adeline. Finch is in Europe becoming a famous concert pianist.

He has not married yet, for Sarah Court, the woman he loves, is still married to his best friend, Arthur Leigh. But Arthur drowns and Sarah is free again. Meanwhile Wakefield Whiteoak, now seventeen, thinks he is falling in love with an impoverished girl named Pauline Lebraux, whose mother is a friend of Renny. Then the family learns that Eden is dying of tuberculosis.

∞

The children were playing at the dining-room table. Mazo was listening to them.

"How do you do, Mr. Brown?" asked Esmée.

"Very well, thank you, Mrs. Brown," replied René.

"I'm not Mrs. Brown. I'm Mrs. Jones."

"Then I'm Mr. Jones."

"You can't be! You're a visitor. "

"Oh!"

"Have you brought your children to London?"

"Oh, yes."

"How many have you, Mr. Brown?"

"Oh, I have ninety eleven, Mrs. Brown."

"I'm not Mrs. Brown! I'm Mrs. Jones."

"Oh!"

"Are you going to call me Mrs. Brown again?"

"Yes"

"Then I'll smack you!"

"I'll fow you in the fire!"

"I'll bite your head off!"

"Mrs. Brown! Mrs. Brown!"

"Stop it!"

Mazo, barely able to contain her laughter, rushed to her study to write down the hilarious dialogue. She would use it in *Beside a Norman Tower.*

⚭

When Mazo finished a novel, she was always restless, eager for a change of scene. Thus, after Mazo finished *The Master of Jalna*, the whole family visited London. There Mazo and Caroline met famous writers like John Galsworthy, and Nurse took the children to see the changing of the guard at Buckingham Palace. Then Mazo and Caroline took a brief trip to Scotland while the children stayed home with the servants. But finally, in the spring of 1933, Mazo's restlessness was so great that only a trip to Canada would do. Mazo, Caroline, a nanny, and the children sailed from Southampton in fair weather on the twentieth of May. Back in Ontario, they moved into a large house in Erindale near Trail Cottage for the summer.

Unfortunately, while on a shopping expedition to Oakville, Caroline was in a car accident and sustained serious injuries to a wrist, a leg, her head, and her back. Then a few months later, when she was still recuperating, she fell and broke her leg again. Rather than returning to England in the autumn, as they had planned, the family moved to Toronto and settled into a large house on Castle Frank Road. Here Esmée and René saw snow for the first time. They tobogganed over the snowdrifts on their front lawn. They made snowmen. Meanwhile, Mazo worked on a new novel: *Young Renny.*

In this fifth Whiteoak novel Mazo would surprise her publishers and her readers. For the first time, she would interrupt the orderly chronological sequence established in *Jalna* and *Whiteoaks of Jalna*. She would go back to before 1924, when *Jalna* begins. *Young Renny* would be set in 1906.

Renny is just eighteen. His twenty-year-old sister Meg is engaged to marry the young man next door: Maurice Vaughan. Renny and Meg do not like their stepmother, Mary Whiteoak. They feel closer to their grandmother, Gran Whiteoak. Renny's father, Philip Whiteoak Junior, is alive. Eden is a boy of five. Piers is a baby nicknamed "Peep" who is teething. Uncle Nick and Uncle Ernest, in their fifties, have squandered their inheritances abroad on high living and dubious speculation respectively, and now they are freeloading at Jalna. Into this situation come two outsiders who cause trouble at Jalna. A gypsy woman seduces Renny. A distant cousin from Ireland befriends Gran, moves into Jalna, and spies on the family...

Mazo's work on *Young Renny* was interrupted when she received word that Nancy Price, a well-known English actress, needed her help in developing a play based on the first two Jalna books. The play was to be mounted very soon on the London stage, and so, in January 1934, Mazo and Caroline made a quick, cold trip by ship to England. They did what they could to help, discovered that the play actually would not be mounted any time soon, and returned to Canada. Then in the warm months they moved back to England with the children. This time they chose to live at The Winnings, a large house near Wales, set in beautiful surroundings.

"We had found nothing that absolutely suited us when, one lovely Autumn day, we heard of a house in the Malvern Hills that had once belonged to a famous engineer," wrote Mazo in a magazine article about The Winnings. "We motored to it and lost our hearts to its garden. In truth, we scarcely looked at the house we were so captivated by the grounds. There were seven acres of them, all little hills and valleys. There were hundreds of trees."

At The Winnings, work resumed on *Young Renny* as well as on the play *Whiteoaks*. When Mazo sent the manuscript of *Young Renny* to her American publisher, the editors criticized the book severely and pointed out how risky it was "to turn back the clock in Jalna." Mazo's response to this new criticism was to show new self-confidence. She told the editors that if they didn't like her work she would take it elsewhere. The editors responded with a soothing letter saying the book was just splendid. Mazo was a goldmine that the publisher could not afford to lose.

☜

In 1935, the year that *Young Renny* was published and work on *Whiteoak Harvest* begun, a Hollywood film company called RKO released a movie based on *Jalna*. The film starred Ian Hunter as Renny, Peggy Wood as Meg, and Jessie Ralph as Gran. Of course Mazo and Caroline went to see the movie. Their feelings about it were mixed.

They felt that the cast was "excellent"… except for Jessie Ralph. "Not one of the attributes that made old

Adeline Whiteoak notable belonged to the actress who played the part," complained Mazo.

They were also angry about a bedroom scene between Meg Whiteoak and Maurice Vaughan. In this scene, Maurice is drinking heavily. Maurice and Meg, sitting well apart, are discussing their past and future. This scene was in questionable taste, according to Mazo and Caroline. What's more, it was not in the novel *Jalna*. Someone in the movie company had invented it!

Not until the play *Whiteoaks* was mounted was Mazo happy with an adaptation of her writing to another medium.

11

Stage Struck and Royalty Mad

I strained toward Windsor, toward the house I owned, from which I should never again be parted.

"Lord, I can almost hear Gran talking!" exclaimed the lanky teenager to his lean but powerfully built older brother.

Two Whiteoak brothers, dark-haired Finch and red-haired Renny, were standing at the open door of a dimly lit, thickly carpeted and curtained bedroom that smelled of camphor and hair oil. On the old leather bed, the head of which was painted with oriental fruit and the grinning faces of two monkeys, perched a green and red parrot. Normally the parrot would have been swearing at the intruders with Hindu curses, but now it was silent.

Vale House near Windsor Castle in the late 1930s.

Mazo, Caroline, and the children lived in this beautiful mansion during their last years in England.

"Can't you hear her Renny?" asked Finch. "'What's going on?'" she's saying. "'I won't be left out of things!'"

"Yes... Yes... She seems to be with us," agreed Renny.

"God! What courage!" croaked Finch.

Renny studied Finch for a moment.

"Don't you realize, Finch, that you've got it too? Clever old Gran discovered it and has given you her chance... Now make the most of it. Don't let her down."

With that, Renny turned his back on Finch and walked slowly away. Finch smiled – almost exultantly. He went over to the piano and sat down at it. He laid his hands on the Chinese statue of Kwan Yin. Strength entered him. He dropped his hands to the keyboard. He looked again into Gran's room. He played.

The curtain fell.

The audience applauded politely.

The curtain rose.

There were Renny, Finch, Meg, Wakefield, Piers, Pheasant, Aunt Augusta, Uncle Nicholas, and Uncle Ernest. There was Gran, alive again, spry and vital at one-hundred-and-one years old. Boney the parrot was perched on Gran's shoulder, rending the air with a metallic screech.

The audience applauded more loudly. It kept on applauding through many curtain calls, including one for the author.

The fifty-seven-year-old author of the play, Mazo de la Roche, was almost as shy and awkward as her fictional character Finch Whiteoak. But somehow she managed to get up onto the stage without stumbling and mumbled a brief speech of thanks.

Afterwards, the cast and crew of the play and some friends and relatives – more than sixty people – crowded into the home Mazo had rented in nearby Stafford Place and partied among the many bouquets of flowers she had received that day. Mazo and Caroline didn't get to bed until three in the morning.

But by dawn the cousins were eating breakfast and reading the reviews. Violet the maid had rushed out into the chill damp April air to buy the newspapers. Most of the reviews were favourable. Ivor Brown in *The Observer*, Charles Morgan in *The Times*, and Littlewood in *The Post* were especially enthusiastic.

∽

Thus went the opening night of the first Canadian play to be staged in the prestigious West End theatre district of London, England. The opening took place on April 13, 1936. The play was called *Whiteoaks*. It was based mainly on Mazo's second Jalna novel, *Whiteoaks of Jalna*. The play was a thrill for Mazo, but it took her on a roller coaster of emotions.

Despite the enthusiastic applause and good reviews, the play's director and lead actress, Nancy Price, soon announced that *Whiteoaks* was to be cancelled. It was just not successful enough. The audiences were not big enough.

What a disappointment! After years of waiting and months of working! Rewrite after rewrite! Price had searched several years for a theatre manager who would mount the play. Mazo had written several more books before Price finally got the Little Theatre in the Adelphi!

Then suddenly Price changed her mind about cancelling. The great George Bernard Shaw had praised Mazo's play! Price transferred *Whiteoaks* to a larger theatre called the Playhouse, and she displayed Shaw's accolade in lights.

London theatre-goers flocked to the play for the next three years until the Second World War, when Nazi bombing made collective evening activities dangerous. People laughed uproariously whenever Gran Whiteoak was on the stage. The Dowager Queen Mary, widow of King George V, went to see the play four or five times and even requested a private meeting with Boney. The play also went to Broadway in New York City, across central Canada, and around England.

More than any single event except the novel *Jalna* winning an international competition, the phenomenal success of the play *Whiteoaks* established Mazo's reputation as a writer.

∞

Rich and famous she had become, but Mazo remained a private person difficult to know well. The English actors and crew of the London production of *Whiteoaks*, with whom she worked closely for months, found her a mystery.

"I thought of her as a detached, insular sort of person," commented Nancy Price. "I mean to say you never knew her."

Although Mazo was excited by the public world of the theatre, she preferred the private world of writing and family. After the uncontrollable emotional ups and downs of *Whiteoaks*, Mazo happily retreated as soon as possible to The Winnings. There she could indulge in the quiet daily routine on which she thrived.

In the morning Mazo had breakfast and then wrote for several hours. Before lunch she went for a walk. In the afternoon she rested for a while, ate a snack that the English called "tea," then spent a few hours with the children. In the evening she had dinner, read aloud to Caroline, or listened while Caroline read aloud to her. The women read either from Mazo's own writing – whatever she had been working on that morning – or from other people's writing.

As Mazo relaxed in this calm, orderly life, she began to think it was finally time to actually buy a house in England, instead of merely renting. Caroline agreed and the two went searching. What a house they found!

The house had been restored by the former owner. There were lawns, a gazebo, an orchard, a lily pond, a sunken garden, greenhouses, and about eight hectares of pastures with Jersey cows grazing.

This was Vale House, a beautiful mansion more than three hundred years old, built in the time of Queen Elizabeth I. Vale House was almost next door to Windsor Castle, one of the royal residences of the king and queen of England. Since King Edward VIII had recently given up the throne, the neighbours were King George VI, his wife, the Queen Consort, and their two young daughters, Princess Elizabeth and

Princess Margaret. (Of course many years later Princess Elizabeth would become Queen Elizabeth II, and her mother, the Queen Consort, would become the Queen Mother, affectionately known as the Queen Mum.)

Almost everybody in the neighbourhood had some connection with the famous upper-class school, Eton, also located nearby, or with Windsor Castle. One friend used to arrive at the gate of Vale House on a handsome grey horse named Silver Mist, followed by two golden retrievers. Mazo and her family regularly received invitations to watch royal functions. Back in Canada her ancestors might have been "distinguished looking nobodies," as Mazo once described them, but here in England Mazo was a *somebody*.

There was always something to do in Windsor. Paxton the chauffeur would drive the family to Chobham Common, to Burnham Beeches, or to Ascot, where Mazo and Caroline could walk and the children and dogs could run free. At the time of the Ascot Races, the children liked to be taken to a spot in Windsor Great Park where they could see the royal family sweep past on the way to the races. One day they were caught in a rain shower.

"Mummy, can't I get out of the car and stand on the grass to see the little princesses?" asked René, who was seven.

"But you'll get wet and you can see the little princesses quite well from the car," objected Mazo.

"I know," René answered firmly, "but they wouldn't see *me*."

∞

Mazo had not been in Vale House for more than two weeks before she began a new novel, *Growth of a Man*. This novel was a sort of vacation for Mazo. Although she was living in England, the novel was set in Canada, mostly among people and places she had known or heard about in early childhood.

Writing *Growth of a Man* gave Mazo her first opportunity to write about the Children of Peace: the unique Quaker group to which Grandma Lundy's family had belonged.

The Children of Peace had been founded by David Willson, a great-uncle of Grandma Lundy. David Willson broke away from traditional Quaker ways. He introduced music to the silent Quaker service. He also preached.

"David Willson gathered the pioneers about him and preached to them under the open sky," Mazo wrote. "The autumn weather was benign, the crops had been bountiful. He stood there, dominant and strong, pouring out the noble words of the Old Testament, words of promise, of might, of peace."

Under David Willson's direction, the Children of Peace built a beautiful place of worship named Sharon Temple. Grandma Lundy's father, Hiram Willson, helped to build it, as did Grandma Lundy's maternal grandfather, Murdoch McLeod.

"The Temple rose in three cubes," Mazo wrote, "one standing above the other, and on the top-most cube a golden ball was to be raised and sheltered beneath a cupola. The Temple was to be painted white for purity. It was to have light from windows on every side, typifying Reason and Truth. Inside there were twelve pillars bearing the names of the twelve apostles..."

Mazo had seen Sharon Temple often as a child. It was located in the village of Sharon, just six or seven kilometres north of Newmarket.

In *Growth of a Man*, Mazo evoked the distant and colourful past of the Willson clan in order to provide a suitable background for a story about a dynamic, modern-day Willson: Harvey Reginald MacMillan, a cousin of Mazo and Caroline. Reggie MacMillan was a grandson of Grandma Lundy's oldest brother, Wellington Willson. He was a great-grandson of Hiram Willson. He was also a founder of the great forestry industry, MacMillan Bloedel Limited of British Columbia.

Growth of a Man is a rags-to-riches story, very different from any of the Jalna novels.

Shaw Manifold, the main character in *Growth of a Man*, begins life as a poor boy. Shaw's father dies and his mother must leave him behind with his grandparents, the Gowers, while she works as a housekeeper to support him. Shaw endures loneliness and cruelty. He labours long hours on his grandparents' farm. He studies hard, overcomes illness, marries his faithful childhood sweetheart, and builds a great industry.

Shaw Manifold was Harvey Reginald MacMillan, more or less. The Gowers were the Willsons, more or less. Cousin Reggie had been raised on Wellington Willson's farm. The fictional setting of most of the novel's early chapters was based on the real Wellington

Willson farm located about four kilometres south of Newmarket in what is the town of Aurora today.

In *Growth of a Man*, Grandfather Gower is cold and mean: "The old man stood solid and imperturbable, his wide-open, china-blue eyes staring above his massive grizzled beard. His hands, leathery and thickened by hard work, hung impassively at his sides."

Shaw Manifold is not very charming either: "He resolutely nursed his grievance against his grandfather, keeping it as a barrier between him and the loss of his mother." But at least Shaw acquires a fortune through his own hard work at hard jobs such as inspecting trees on horseback in bad weather in the wilderness of the Canadian West.

Growth of a Man did not receive the Governor General's Award in 1938, but the novel was a close contender for this prestigious annual prize, given for the first time in 1937.

And in 1938 Mazo was awarded the Lorne Pierce Medal. This gold-plated, silver medal was awarded once a year to one person. It was given by the Royal Society of Canada for an achievement of special significance and conspicuous merit in imaginative or critical literature written in either English or French.

Today Sharon Temple is a national historic site. MacMillan Bloedel Limited became Canada's largest forest-products company.

∞

In the fall of 1938, Mazo had an operation on her throat to remove a cyst. The operation was successful, but she was slow in recovering her full health.

By the spring of 1939, Mazo, Caroline, and the children had been living at Vale House for two years. René was eight and getting difficult to manage. He needed to go to a regular school instead of being taught at home by a governess. There had been rumours of war for several years, but now gas masks were being issued, and Esmée, who was ten, was frightened by the masks. Perhaps it was time to return to Canada for a while. There the family would find sunshine and peace. They loved Vale House, and they loved England, but it was time to leave – just for a while.

∽

"You would think the end of the world had come!" exclaimed Mazo, bringing a cup of hot tea to Caroline, who was in bed with the flu. Today was the maid's day off, and the children were away at school. "Here it is March, and we have not seen the bare ground since early November. And the snow is falling fast."

"This winter has broken a record that stood fifty years," said Caroline, sitting up in bed to drink her tea. "Even for Canada, it is severe. I long for balmy old England."

"Put that blanket around your shoulders, or you'll be sick for another week, and I can't cope alone," said Mazo. "You should have seen me going to the poultry house through the drifts, carrying kettles of boiling water to thaw the buckets, which were solid ice. The hens seemed not too unhappy though. They even managed a little song."

"We are like pioneers in the wilderness here in York Mills," commented Caroline, between sips of her tea. "Zero weather now seems nothing to us. Thirty below is the norm."

"If there is anything we should be grateful for now, it is having congenial work to do that is quite outside the war," returned Mazo.

"We have had fun this year with *The Building of Jalna*," said Caroline. "The years 1853 and 1854 were so tranquil compared to 1942 and 1943!"

"There were times when I forgot the present and lived only in those long-ago years," said Mazo. "I wonder what the early settlers would have thought if they could have seen the Ontario of today?"

∞

Although Mazo complained about the severe winters in Canada, she was grateful that she and her family could live in safety during the Second World War. As she wrote *The Building of Jalna*, about the founding of Jalna in the 1850s, she was well aware of what was happening in Europe. Often, in the evenings, she and Caroline sat tensely in front of the radio, inwardly shaken by terrible news such as the bombing of London and the fall of France. Mazo included references to the war in her novels *Wakefield's Course* and *Return to Jalna*, written during this period also. In Europe during the Second World War, Mazo was the only known Canadian author. Actually, to some people in Germany, Mazo's books were treasured secret possessions that represented the struggle against fascism. The Whiteoak family was English, and this fact reminded anti-Nazis of the sunshine of freedom that shone beyond the shadow of Hitler.

∞

When Mazo, Caroline, and the children moved to Canada in 1939, Mazo was sixty years old. She had written six Jalna novels. In the next two decades she would write ten more Jalna novels. She would also write a number of other books, including a novel, a novella, a history of Quebec City, several short children's books, a play, and her autobiography. She did all this writing in Canada. Except for a few brief visits, she never returned to England.

From 1939 to 1945, Mazo and her family lived successively in three houses in the Toronto area. The first was in the village of Thornhill, just north of Toronto. The second, called "Windrush Hill," was located at the junction of Bayview Avenue and Steeles Avenue in York Mills, now part of Toronto. The third was on Russell Hill Road, right in Toronto.

In 1946, the British government expropriated Vale House, Mazo's home in England, and Mazo and Caroline sold Trail Cottage. In 1953 the family moved into 3 Ava Crescent in the posh Forest Hill district of Toronto. There Mazo and Caroline stayed until their deaths.

This last home in Forest Hill was as English as it could be. Large and rambling, with Tudor-style timbers, a panelled entrance, snug library, terrace, and deep fireplace, it had badly heated, undecorated servants' quarters on the top floor.

Mazo de la Roche at about eighty.

12

Endings

This latest period of mine is mostly a record of books written, of seeing my children grow up, of seeing a different sort of world arise to my astonished view.

"Meals at certain times," muttered Esmée. "Have lunch. Have tea... They read out loud to each other. They go for walks. You know what time it is when they call the dogs. They go to bed at the same time every day... Of course they have a cook and a maid, so naturally the meals have to be on time, but I wonder why they can't have some freedom.

"Mazo writes from 10 until noon every day. She isn't a flexible person. It was her upbringing. Her grandparents were staid. Everything she knows she was taught by her grandparents. She was terribly protected.

"She doesn't know how to cope with the outside world. She has a few friends, but not so many. I feel sorry for her. She's missing a lot of what the world is about."

∞

During the final two decades of her life, Mazo experienced some personal troubles that marred her otherwise contented and productive life. Now and then Caroline was ill. Sometimes Mazo was ill: now the flu, now a kidney infection, eventually Parkinson's disease and rheumatoid arthritis. Occasionally Mazo had troubles with servants. Sometimes she worried about René or clashed with Esmée.

After the family moved to Canada, Esmée and René both attended private boarding schools and summer camps, so they were never home for long. Both children married in 1953, and René was soon a father. Eventually he had three children.

René always felt close to Mazo. Yet, when he was a child he showed signs of being somewhat unhappy, for he was neither a good student nor a good mixer. And when he was a man he was rather unstable. For example, he married three times.

After René dropped out of university to get married for the first time, Mazo tried to help him find a good job. On René's behalf, Mazo wrote to important men.

Mazo wrote to her friend and long-time editor Rache Lovat Dickson in 1954: "As for René, he is working with a Belgian engineer and a gang of French Canadians, making a road through a forest, eighty-five miles north of his home. It has been a wet cold summer and he is soaked through most of the time and is sleeping under canvas."

Mazo asked in this letter whether Mr. Lovat Dickson, a director and the general editor of her British publisher, Macmillan, could give René a letter of introduction to take to author and scientist C.P. Snow, a director of English Electric, who was visiting Canada on business. Mazo hoped Mr. Snow would give René a better job.

Mr. Snow met René. But Mr. Snow did not give René a job.

Eventually, through a contact at the Canadian Broadcasting Corporation, Mazo got René a job in a cement-making firm.

Meanwhile Esmée felt alienated from Mazo and Caroline. Esmée felt the women had discarded her like an unwanted toy when she ceased to be a cute child. She thought Mazo and Caroline were too old to understand her.

Although Mazo and Caroline were generous with their money in many ways, they made Esmée wear their hand-me-down clothing. The clothing had been made over for Esmée by a seamstress, but it still looked strange. She had to go to a high-school formal looking like a Kate Greenaway character! So Esmée felt.

Esmée also saw the women's life as too regimented. She left home when she was eighteen. She didn't see the family much after her marriage. At Christmastime she would put in an appearance.

∞

Mazo also had some professional troubles. Or so she felt. She often complained that her work was dismissed by her fellow countrymen while it was praised abroad, especially in England. This had been true in the case of *Delight* in 1926, but it was not true after the third Jalna novel appeared. After the publication in 1931 of *Finch's Fortune*, reviewers in Canada did not differ from reviewers in the United States and Britain. On both sides of the Atlantic, most reviewers doubted that the quality of the series could be maintained if there were too many sequels.

Yet some intelligent, well-read Canadians were still praising Mazo's work. For example, in 1940 novelist and critic Robertson Davies wrote that Mazo was "that rare creature in the literary world, a born storyteller."

When *The Building of Jalna* was published in 1944, one British book critic wrote: "It does not contain a single line or a single idea to prompt any serious thought." Other British critics made similarly disparaging remarks.

After the Second World War, most Canadian reviewers saved their highest praise for the rising stars of Canadian literature. They lauded Hugh MacLennan, whose *Two Solitudes* won the Governor General's Award in 1945. They raved about Gabrielle Roy, whose *Tin Flute* won the Governor General's Award in 1947.

But in 1951 Mazo received a silver medal from the University of Alberta. Mazo was the first recipient of this national award, which was established to honour

Canadians whose careers had contributed greatly to literature, painting, or music. Furthermore, in 1954 Mazo received an honorary degree from the University of Toronto.

Also, Mazo's books continued to sell well in Canada and abroad. The critics might have mocked *The Building of Jalna*, but it was on the *New York Times* bestseller list.

And Mazo continued to enjoy a satisfying relationship with her innumerable readers. She received thousands of fan letters from all over the world in countless languages from individuals with all levels of education. And she replied to many of them herself. Indeed, her own need to keep telling the story of the Whiteoaks was inspired by her fans' need to know more about them.

After the Second World War, in France, Mazo was the most widely read author of any nationality. In communist Poland, Czechoslovakia, and Hungary, pirated editions of her novels circulated widely. In Norway, houses, dogs, and even children were named after the house Jalna or individual members of the Whiteoak family. Indeed, there were houses called "Jalna" in Greece, Australia, Egypt, and the United States! In the U.S., one could buy "Jalna" sneakers. In Canada, streets, restaurants, and schools were named after Mazo and her Jalna books.

In international popularity Mazo was rivalled only by a few female writers of the next generation. One of these rivals was English writer Daphne du Maurier, who had been born in 1907. Du Maurier was the author of *Jamaica Inn*, *Frenchman's Creek*, and *Rebecca*. Another rival was American writer Margaret

Mitchell, born in 1900. Mitchell was the author of *Gone with the Wind*.

Actually, Mazo may have influenced Mitchell. In *Jalna*, a minor character named Miss Pink blushes and turns into "Miss Scarlet." Miss Scarlett is the name of the main character of *Gone with the Wind*. In *Jalna*, Alayne Archer asks her beloved, Renny Whiteoak, whether the time since they last met seems long or short to him. Renny replies, "Gone like the wind."

∞

"Jalna, with its faded red brick, almost covered by vines, its stone porch, its five chimneys, rising from the sloping roof where pigeons eternally cooed and slid, where their droppings defaced the leaves of the Virginia creeper and the window sills, where smoke was always coming out of one or more of the chimneys and where the old wooden shingles so often managed to spring a leak."

So the grand old home of the Whiteoak family is described in *Centenary at Jalna*. Published in 1958, *Centenary* was the fifteenth Jalna book that Mazo wrote. (The sixteenth Jalna novel and the last to be published was *Morning at Jalna*. It was not very good.) *Centenary at Jalna* was set in 1953 and 1954.

Mazo wrote *Centenary*, the proper end of the Jalna series, when she was almost eighty years old. *Centenary* is the story of how the Whiteoaks celebrate the one-hundredth anniversary of the building of their home. Mazo's portrait of the family is sardonic and suggests that this aristocratic tribe is degenerating.

Renny, now past sixty but with few grey hairs, is still the head of the clan. Renny is scheming to celebrate the centennial by marrying his daughter Adeline to his nephew Philip, so the estate will stay in the family. Philip's father Piers (Renny's half-brother) agrees this is a good idea. But Philip's mother, Pheasant, disagrees. So does Adeline's mother, Alayne,

"Who do they think they are?" cries Pheasant. "Arranging other people's lives. Pushing them about like pawns. Why – you'd think Jalna was a dukedom instead of just an Ontario farm!"

Alayne thinks a union between the first cousins would be bizarre and "dangerous."

Heedless of the mothers' wise counsel, the fathers push ahead with their scheme and manage to interest young Adeline and Philip in it too. This stubborn stupidity on the part of Renny and Piers is matched by that of Finch, who is now also the father of a teenager. Finch habitually neglects and even rejects the son he had by Sarah Court, who has been dead for a number of years. This son, Dennis, now thirteen, has developed serious emotional problems that eventually lead to tragedy.

Mazo's portrait of the disturbed Dennis is brilliant, but *Centenary at Jalna* is not all about the darkness of incest and madness. The novel is also about the light of intelligence and love, as well as humour. University student Archer Whiteoak, the younger child of Renny and Alayne, is cold but witty and well able to mock the strange notions of his elders and peers. Eight-year-old Mary Whiteoak, the youngest child of Piers and Pheasant, is well-balanced, charming, and kind. Noah Binns, the ignorant hired man who is always making gloomy predictions, provides comic relief.

By the end of *Centenary at Jalna*, the Whiteoaks seem to be on the verge of disaster, but in the final scene, some hope for the future emerges. Innocent little Mary Whiteoak coos lovingly over Finch's second child, a baby boy whom Finch also neglects. "You're prettier than a spider, sweeter than a rose," sings Mary. This dear little girl will perhaps give new life to the dynasty engendered by her great-grandparents.

∽

Mazo de la Roche died quietly in the early morning of July 12, 1961 at her home in Toronto, in bed in the presence of her family. She had been bedridden and in the care of nurses for several years, but she had been working on a seventeenth Jalna novel – never completed. After Mazo passed away, Caroline immediately went into her own room and closed the door. Later that day she sent a telegram to Mazo's publisher: "MAZO LEFT US LAST NIGHT PLEASE TELL THE OTHERS." She burned Mazo's diaries.

Caroline overrode Mazo's will, which said she should be buried in Toronto. Caroline directed that Mazo be buried in St. George's churchyard beside Sibbald Point Provincial Park on the south shore of Lake Simcoe, near Sutton.

For eleven years Caroline lived on alone in the house on Ava Crescent in Toronto. Along with her fellow executors – René, Esmée, and lawyer Daniel Lang (later Senator Lang) – Caroline dealt with requests regarding Mazo's literary legacy.

Caroline donated most of Mazo's papers to the University of Toronto. Today these papers are stored in boxes in the Thomas Fisher Rare Book Library at the University of Toronto. The boxes take up nine metres of shelf space. The papers include personal and business letters, first editions of her books, fan letters, and original manuscripts.

Caroline also gave interviews to Mazo's first biographer, Ronald Hambleton. And she negotiated television rights for the Jalna series with the Canadian Broadcasting Corporation.

"They think I am just a stupid old woman," said Caroline to the darkness. "No one cares about my opinion."

Caroline was furious. The tiny, elderly woman of ninety-three lay awake in bed for hours on that hot July night in 1971, in her home in Toronto. She who had been the model for the beautiful young Alayne Archer had lived nearly as long as Gran Whiteoak! And now she would dearly like to thrash someone with her cane, like Gran used to do.

"How dare they?" Caroline muttered. "And now nothing can be done to stop them! It's a good thing that Mazo is dead! She would have been terribly upset!"

Suddenly Caroline felt a presence in the room. She turned her head toward the presence. It was Gigi, the honey-coloured cat that had arrived on their doorstep as a kitten when Mazo was still alive.

"Those people from the Canadian Broadcasting Corporation were so underhanded," Caroline said to Gigi. "They plied me with flowers, talking books, and music cassettes. They sent my favourite music to listen to during the long hours that I am alone. I shall never listen to anything produced by the CBC again!"

Gigi jumped up on the bed to be petted.

"I lie awake at night quite often, Gigi, and I can't read any more because my eyesight is so poor," said Caroline. "That's why I listen to CBC Radio. I'm awfully lonely, Gigi. I do wish Mazo were still with us."

Gigi purred.

"But I didn't go to the screening tonight!" exclaimed Caroline. "And I told the children and all of our friends not to go either. The CBC types thought I'd be flattered to be invited to the screening, but I wasn't fooled this time. I told them I didn't want to see their stupid 'pilot episode,' or whatever it is called. There is to be hardly a thing from our Jalna books, Gigi.

"They didn't tell me until after I'd signed the contract that they were going to invent new material for the Jalna television shows. They said they wanted to bring the Whiteoaks 'up to date!' Mazo always disliked and distrusted television, and she was right. It's all about American commercialism. Oh, I am so angry!"

Beyond the grey stone crosses, side by side, green leaves rustle and yellow sunlight sparkles on gentle blue waves. On a summer's day the graveyard is lovely. On Mazo's Celtic cross is the traditional French motto of the ancient de la Roche family: "*Mon dieu est ma roche.*" This means "My God is my rock." There is also another sentence: "Death interrupts all that is mortal."

When Caroline died on August 3, 1972, Esmée and René buried her beside Mazo. On Caroline's plain cross is the sentence: "Hand in hand we kept the faith."

Mazo and Caroline rest beside their beloved Lake Simcoe. They are on the southeast side of the lake, as far as possible from where Caroline's family was so unhappy in Orillia. They are near where they vacationed so often – even in old age. They are not far from where their ancestors pioneered. They are in the centre of where it all happened. In all directions of the compass took place the real and imagined events that, with Caroline's help, Mazo made into wonderful stories.

"My books are transmuted reminiscences," Mazo said once. "Whatever I am I have put into my books."

Heather Kirk and Jack Winzer.

Gravestones of Mazo de la Roche and Caroline Clement.

Epilogue

For many decades many Canadian academics have been saying that the Jalna novels are flawed because the Whiteoaks and their way of life are not realistic.

"Mazo de la Roche is a romantic artist. It is her romanticism, I believe, that has made her such an embarrassment to Canadian critics," said one professor, Desmond Pacey.

Mazo created "larger-than-life characters with exaggerated passions," said another professor, George Hendrick.

Mazo created a "myth of a humane, harmless gentry – living in the Canadian Great Good Place," said a third professor, Dennis Duffy.

Yet the Jalna novels have always had defenders among educated people.

"The creation of the Jalna books is the most protracted single feat of literary invention in the brief history of Canada's literature," said literary critic and novelist, Robertson Davies.

The Jalna series covered with "comprehensive detail" a century of enormous change in this country, said a biographer and broadcaster, Ronald Hambleton. The series documented "the decline of an era."

De la Roche's work "forms the transition" between the generation of Margaret Atwood and Margaret Laurence and their "nineteenth-century foremothers," Susanna Moodie and Catharine Parr Traill, said another biographer, Professor Joan Givner.

"The world of Jalna is an integral part of the roots of Canada," said novelist Scott Symons. "To lose it would leave us groping for an abandoned identity."

Academics, literary critics, and creative writers may continue to debate the value of Mazo's work for many more decades, but no one can deny that she was once popular.

By the time Mazo died in 1961, the Jalna series had sold eleven million copies in 193 English-language editions and 92 foreign-language editions.

And today, Mazo is still popular in France. In 1994, France 2, a Paris-based private television station with public-broadcast responsibilities, aired *Jalna*, a TV mini-series based on Mazo's novels. The station spent sixteen million dollars producing the series.

The only other female writer of Mazo's time who lived in Canada and who ultimately enjoyed comparable success to Mazo was Lucy Maud Montgomery, the author of *Anne of Green Gables* and its sequels. Montgomery, born in Prince Edward Island, wrote for children, not adults: a traditional area of strength for women with literary ambitions. Mazo wrote for adults, and she was far more successful in this than most of her male colleagues.

The only *male* writer of Mazo's time who lived in Canada and who ultimately enjoyed comparable success to Mazo was Stephen Butler Leacock. Leacock, who was born in England, was the author of *Sunshine Sketches of a Little Town*. He was another rich and famous Canadian writer who wrote too much too quickly but whose best work is of outstanding literary merit.

Strangely, there is no national heritage site exclusively dedicated to Mazo and her work. L.M. Montgomery has a national heritage site: Green Gables Heritage Place in Prince Edward Island National Park. Stephen Leacock has a national heritage site: the Leacock Museum in Orillia, Ontario. Yet, although Parks Canada has officially designated Mazo as a person of national significance in the arts, only locally administered heritage sites commemorate her.

In 1995, the first local museum partly dedicated to commemorating Mazo was opened: Benares Historic House in Mississauga, Ontario. Benares is administered by the City of Mississauga. In 1996, the second local museum partly dedicated to commemorating Mazo was opened: Sovereign House in Bronte, Ontario. Sovereign House is administered by the Bronte Historical Society.

Perhaps some day a national museum or other such heritage site will be dedicated exclusively to Mazo de la Roche, her life, and her work.

The Jalna Novels
by Mazo de la Roche

In Order of Year of Publication	In Order of Year Story Begins
Jalna 1927	*The Building of Jalna* 1853
Whiteoaks of Jalna 1929	*Morning at Jalna* 1863
Finch's Fortune 1931	*Mary Wakefield* 1894
The Master of Jalna 1933	*Young Renny* 1906
Young Renny 1935	*Whiteoak Heritage* 1918
Whiteoak Harvest 1936	*The Whiteoak Brothers* 1923
Whiteoak Heritage 1940	*Jalna* 1924
Wakefield's Course 1941	*Whiteoaks of Jalna* 1926
The Building of Jalna 1944	*Finch's Fortune* 1929
Return to Jalna 1946	*The Master of Jalna* 1931
Mary Wakefield 1949	*Whiteoak Harvest* 1934
Renny's Daughter 1951	*Wakefield's Course* 1939
The Whiteoak Brothers 1953	*Return to Jalna* 1943
Variable Winds at Jalna 1954	*Renny's Daughter* 1948
Centenary at Jalna 1958	*Variable Winds at Jalna* 1950
Morning at Jalna 1960	*Centenary at Jalna* 1953

Other Books
by Mazo de la Roche

In Order of Date of Publication

Explorers of the Dawn 1922 (short stories)
Possession 1923 (novel)
Low Life 1925 (play)
Delight 1926 (novel)
Come True 1927 (play)
Return of the Emigrant 1928 (play)
Portrait of a Dog 1930 (biography)
Lark Ascending 1932 (novel)
The Thunder of New Wings 1932 (novel)
Beside a Norman Tower 1934 (fictionalized biography)
Whiteoaks 1936 (play)
The Very House 1937 (fictionalized biography)
Growth of a Man 1938 (novel)
The Sacred Bullock and Other Stories of Animals 1939 (short stories)
The Two Saplings 1942 (novel)
Quebec: Historic Seaport 1945 (non-fiction)
Mistress of Jalna 1951 (play)
A Boy in the House 1952 (novella)
Song of Lambert 1955 (children's book – fiction)
Ringing the Changes 1957 (autobiography)
Bill and Coo 1958 (children's book – fiction)

Mazo de la Roche and Caroline Clement,
visiting Bronte in the 1930s.

Chronology of Mazo de la Roche (1879-1961)

Compiled by Clarence Karr

MAZO DE LA ROCHE AND HER TIMES	CANADA AND THE WORLD
1812 John and Titus Willson, great-great-uncles of Mazo de la Roche, take part in the War of 1812 on the British side; John Willson fights in the Battle of Queenston Heights and receives a medal for bravery.	**1812** The United States declares war on Britain. British General Isaac Brock dies in battle at Queenston Heights on the Niagara Peninsula and becomes a Canadian hero.
1814 Mazo de la Roche's paternal grandfather, John Richmond Roche, is born in Limerick County, Ireland. He will emigrate to North America as a young man. The Battle of Lundy's Lane takes place near the Niagara farm of William Lundy, a first cousin of	**1814** The Treaty of Ghent is signed on 14 December, ending the war between Britain and the United States. The major battles occurred on British North American soil in what are now the provinces of Ontario and Quebec.

Mazo de la Roche

MAZO DE LA ROCHE AND HER TIMES	CANADA AND THE WORLD

Mazo's great-great-grandfather, Enos Lundy.

1826
Sarah Bryan, Mazo's paternal grandmother, is born in Dublin, Ireland. Her parents bring her to British North America as a baby.

1826
Construction begins on the Rideau Canal, a British military project linking Bytown and Kingston. Prior to Confederation Bytown is renamed Ottawa as the capital of the United Canadas.

1827
Daniel Lundy, Mazo's maternal grandfather, is born in Whitchurch Township, York County, Upper Canada, now the province of Ontario.

1831
Louise Willson, maternal grandmother of Mazo, is born in East Gwillimbury Township, York County. The Willsons are members of a breakaway Quaker group, the Children of Peace.

1831
Susanna Strickland marries John Dunbar Moodie in London, England. The next year the family, with one child, moves to Upper Canada.

The Children of Peace complete the building of Sharon Temple.

1848
John Roche marries Sarah Bryan.

1852
William Roche, father of Mazo de la Roche, is born, probably in Belleville, Canada West, now the province of Ontario.

1852
Susanna Moodie publishes what will become her best-known book, *Roughing It in the Bush*. It records her experiences in the transition from a middle-class life in England to the frontier life of a settler in the backwoods of Upper Canada.

Rich and Famous Writer

MAZO DE LA ROCHE AND HER TIMES

1853
Louise Willson marries Daniel Lundy.

1854
Alberta Lundy, mother of Mazo, is born to Louise and Daniel Lundy.

1865
John Roche, grandfather of Mazo, is living in Baltimore, Maryland. His wife and children are living in Whitby, Ontario.

CANADA AND THE WORLD

1853
Moodie's sequel, *Life in the Clearings*, which depicts town life in Belleville, appears in print.

1854
A Reciprocity Treaty inaugurates free trade between the British North American colonies and the U.S.

1857
Atlantic Monthly is founded and quickly assumes a position as the most respected literary periodical in the U.S.

1865
Abraham Lincoln, sixteenth president of the United States, is assassinated.

The U.S. Civil War ends.

1867
The British North America Act establishes the Dominion of Canada, uniting Nova Scotia, New Brunswick, Quebec, and Ontario. John A. Macdonald is elected prime minister and is knighted by Queen Victoria.

1868
Agnes Fitzgibbon and Catharine Parr Traill publish *Canadian Wild Flowers*, one of the first coloured depictions of this aspect of Canadian nature.

Mazo de la Roche

MAZO DE LA ROCHE AND HER TIMES	CANADA AND THE WORLD

1876

Daniel Lundy moves his wife and children from Bradford, Ontario to Newmarket, Ontario. Danford Roche moves his mother and brothers from Whitby to Newmarket. Danford opens a dry goods store. His brother William works in the store and courts Alberta Lundy, whom he will soon marry.

1878

Caroline Louise Clement is born to Martha and James Clement on April 4 in Innisfil Township.

1879

Mazo Louise Roche, later changed to de la Roche, is born to Alberta and William Roche on January 15 in the home of her maternal grandparents in Newmarket, Ontario. Her mother will suffer from ill health for most of her life. Grandmother Louise Lundy will handle most of the parental responsibilities.

1876

Famed Canadian soprano Emma Albani, from Quebec, continues to impress audiences in Europe. It is only a year ago that she first sang at Covent Garden, London.

Dr. Emily Stowe founds the Toronto Women's Literary Club.

1878

George Reid, eighteen years old, moves to Toronto to study at the Ontario School of Art under Robert Harris.

Sir John A. Macdonald and his Conservative party win the general election. He promises a new national policy involving completion of the Pacific railway, tariff protection, and increased immigration.

1879

Ethel Barrymore, actress and film star, is born in New York City. She will play the leading role in the New York production of *Whiteoaks*, based on a Mazo de la Roche novel.

The world's first artificial ice surface opens in Madison Square Gardens in New York.

MAZO DE LA ROCHE AND HER TIMES

1880
Grandfather John Roche dies of heat prostration in Baltimore, Maryland. Danford Roche brings his father's body and books to Newmarket.

1887
Mazo Roche and Caroline Clement meet for the first time. Because of adverse family circumstances they will spend most of the rest of their childhoods together in the Lundy household. The two will live together as adults until the death of Mazo.

1888
The Lundy household moves to Orillia.

1890
Mazo and Caroline are attending a private school in Orillia.

1891
Mazo moves to a Galt, Ontario hotel with her mother and father. Caroline remains in Orillia, living temporarily with her parents.

CANADA AND THE WORLD

1880
A contract for the construction of a railway from Montreal to the Pacific is awarded to the Canadian Pacific Railway syndicate. Upon its completion five years later, the railway becomes a central link in the forging of a national market. This is especially important for the book trade. Salesmen from Toronto-based publishers call upon their retail stores twice a year.

1887
In the Canadian federal election John A. Macdonald and the Conservatives are returned with a reduced majority.

Buffalo Bill's Wild West Show opens in London, England on May 9.

1890
William Arthur Deacon, who will become dean of Canadian literary critics, is born in Pembroke, Ontario.

1891
Canadian Prime Minister John A. Macdonald dies in office.

Frederick Banting, co-discoverer of insulin for the control of diabetes, is born at Alliston, Ontario.

Mazo de la Roche

MAZO DE LA ROCHE AND HER TIMES	CANADA AND THE WORLD
1892 Mazo and her mother return to Orillia and the household of Daniel Lundy. Mazo's father drifts from job to job and place to place.	**1892** Movie actress Mary Pickford is born in Toronto. The Toronto *Star* newspaper is founded.
1894 The Lundy household, including Mazo and her parents, moves to the Parkdale district of Toronto. Mazo will attend Parkdale Collegiate and study piano at the Metropolitan School of Music. Caroline rejoins the Lundy household.	**1894** In England, Hugh Eayrs, future president of Macmillan Canada, is born. Robert Louis Stevenson, Scottish author of *Treasure Island, The Strange Case of Dr. Jekyll and Mr. Hyde*, and other classics, dies.
1897 Mazo and Caroline are enjoying most of the normal activities of young women their age.	**1897** Wilfrid Laurier, prime minister of Canada, is knighted as part of the Queen Victoria's Diamond Jubilee celebrations. George A. Reid is elected president of the Ontario Society of Artists.
1899 Mazo is taking occasional classes at the University of Toronto	**1899** A Canadian bestseller fiction list begins on a monthly tally basis. Bestseller lists in both Britain and the U.S. have preceded the Canadian one by four years. The Boer War begins in South Africa. Canadian men will volunteer to serve in the British army.

MAZO DE LA ROCHE AND HER TIMES	CANADA AND THE WORLD
1900 Daniel Lundy dies. Mazo's father, William Roche, moves the Lundy household from Parkdale to fashionable Jarvis Street in central Toronto.	
1901 William Roche returns to his pattern of moving from place to place in the Toronto region. Now Alberta, Mazo, and Caroline go with him. Mazo attends classes at the Ontario School of Art under the direction of George A. Reid.	**1901** In Britain, Queen Victoria dies and is succeeded by her son, Edward VII. Canadian author Gilbert Parker achieves a number four position on the American bestseller list for fiction with *The Right of Way*. Marconi transmits telegraphic radio messages from Cornwall, England to Newfoundland.
1902 Mazo tries writing. She publishes a short story in *Munsey's* magazine.	**1902** The Boer War ends with a hard-fought British victory.
1903 During this period Mazo experiences a nervous collapse.	**1903** In the U.S., Orville and Wilbur Wright successfully fly their airplane, *Kitty Hawk*. Henry Ford founds the Ford Motor Company. Lou Gehrig, American baseball player, is born. His name will be used for a fatal disease of the nervous system.
1905 Mazo's father purchases a hotel in Acton, Ontario and his family moves to that town.	**1905** The Macmillan publishing house sends Frank Wise to Toronto to establish a branch of the New York office.

MAZO DE LA ROCHE AND HER TIMES	CANADA AND THE WORLD
	British author Ethel C. Mayne publishes her influential biography of Romantic poet, Lord Byron.
1906 Mazo and Caroline are often seen driving around Acton in a two-wheeled cart pulled by a Shetland pony. Mazo is writing stories.	**1906** British writer John Galsworthy publishes *The Forsyte Saga*, the first in a series of novels centred on the lives of the Forsyte family.
1907 Mazo publishes a short story in H.L. Mencken's avant-garde magazine, *Smart Set*.	**1907** Rudyard Kipling, famed British poet and storyteller, is awarded the Nobel Prize in Literature.
	Canadian author Ralph Connor's novel, *The Doctor*, reaches eighth position on the American best-seller list.
	1909 George A. Reid becomes Director of the Central Ontario School of Art and Design.
	Poet Dorothy Livesay is born in Winnipeg.
	The Canadian bestseller list for this year includes Nellie McClung's *Sowing Seeds in Danny* in number four position, L.M. Montgomery's *Anne of Green Gables* number six, and her *Anne of Avonlea* in eighth place.
	Canadian poet A.M. Klein is born in the Russian Ukraine to an orthodox Jewish family.

MAZO DE LA ROCHE AND HER TIMES	CANADA AND THE WORLD
1910 Mazo publishes a short story called "Spirit of the Dance" in *The Canadian Magazine*.	**1910** L.M. Montgomery's *Kilmeny of the Orchard* reaches number two position on the Canadian bestseller list. In Britain, King Edward VII dies and is succeeded by his son George V.
1911 William Roche leases a fruit farm near Bronte beside Lake Ontario. He, Alberta, Mazo, and Caroline move to this location and try farming. Mazo publishes a short story called "Canadian Ida and English Nell" in *The Metropolitan*. Mazo's paternal grandmother, Sarah Roche, dies in Newmarket.	**1911** Marie Curie wins the Nobel Prize for Chemistry.
1912 Mazo meets a young French engineer named Pierre Fritz Mansbendel, who is boarding with Mazo's Aunt Eva in Toronto. Pierre and Mazo will remain lifelong friends.	**1912** Hugh Eayrs arrives in Toronto from England to work for the publishing house Macmillan Co. of Canada. Stephen Leacock's *Sunshine Sketches of a Little Town* is in tenth place on the Canadian bestseller list.
1913 Mazo's maternal grandmother, Louise Lundy, dies in Toronto.	**1913** Woodrow Wilson becomes President of the United States.

MAZO DE LA ROCHE AND HER TIMES	CANADA AND THE WORLD
1914	**1914**
William Roche gives up the farm. This experiment has ended in bankruptcy.	The First World War begins.
	The Panama Canal opens.
Mazo publishes a story in *Atlantic Monthly* magazine.	A new edition of Susanna Moodie's *Roughing It in the Bush* reaches number eight on the
Pierre Fritz Mansbendel marries Mazo's Aunt Eva and moves to New York City.	Canadian non-fiction bestseller list.
1915	**1915**
William Roche dies in Bronte. Mazo, Alberta, and Caroline move to Toronto, where Caroline begins working as a clerk in the provincial parliament buildings to support the family.	L.M. Montgomery's *Anne of the Island* is number eight on the Canadian bestseller list.
	In Belgium, Canadian troops fight their first major battle at Ypres.
1917	**1917**
Caroline becomes a statistician in the Fire Marshall's office of the Ontario government.	The Russian Revolution overthrows the imperial government of the czar and places the Bolsheviks in power.
	1918
	The First World War ends.
1919	**1919**
Mazo is writing humorous short stories.	J.F.B. Livesay, husband of Florence and father of Dorothy, publishes a best-selling volume on
Mazo and Caroline spend their summer vacation with Mazo's mother, Alberta. They stay in their usual spot on the shore of Lake Simcoe in Innisfil Township.	the First World War entitled *Canada's Hundred Days*. He becomes general manager of the Canadian Press news service.
Caroline's brother dies.	Peter McArthur's biography of Sir Wilfrid Laurier reaches number

MAZO DE LA ROCHE AND HER TIMES	CANADA AND THE WORLD
	eight on the Canadian non-fiction bestseller list.
	Ralph Connor's *Sky Pilot in No Man's Land* achieves number five position on the American bestseller list for fiction.
1920 Mazo's mother dies of influenza.	**1920** The Group of Seven Canadian artists forms in Toronto. Members are: A.Y. Jackson; Frank Johnston; Lawren Harris; Franklin Carmichael; F.H. Varley; Arthur Lismer; and J.E.H. MacDonald.
1921 Mazo begins writing a novel and some plays.	**1921** The Canadian Authors Association is created in Montreal. Most Canadian authors, including Mazo de la Roche, will become members.
	William Lyon Mackenzie King is elected prime minister of Canada.
	Hugh Eayrs assumes the presidency of Macmillan of Canada.
1922 Mazo publishes her first book, *Explorers of the Dawn*, a collection of stories. This book, published by Knopf, becomes a bestseller in the U.S. Mazo visits Nova Scotia and writes her second novel, *The Thunder of New Wings*.	**1922** Nellie McClung's highly political novel, *Purple Springs*, is number nine on the Canadian bestseller list. W.A. Deacon begins his literary journalism career with *Saturday Night* magazine in Toronto.

MAZO DE LA ROCHE AND HER TIMES	CANADA AND THE WORLD
Caroline and Mazo become friends of the Livesay family and purchase property beside the Livesay home in Clarkson, Ontario, just west of Toronto.	The Ottawa Film Productions movie, *The Man From Glengarry*, based on the Ralph Connor novel, is released.
1923 Mazo and Caroline spend their first summer in their newly constructed cottage in Clarkson. Mazo works on her third novel, *Delight*. Mazo publishes her first novel, *Possession*, with Macmillan.	**1923** Canadians Frederick Banting and John Macleod win the Nobel Prize for Medicine for the discovery of insulin, which extends and improves the lives of victims of diabetes. *Time* magazine is launched. In Britain, the future King George VI and Queen Elizabeth are married in Westminster Abbey.
1925 Mazo's play *Low Life* is produced. Mazo begins to write *Jalna*, the novel that will introduce the Whiteoak family. The Whiteoaks live in southern Ontario in a big, old, red-brick house called Jalna.	**1925** British dramatist George Bernard Shaw wins the Nobel Prize in Literature. W.A. Deacon creates a "Literary Section" in *Saturday Night* magazine.
1926 Mazo publishes her novel *Delight*. Mazo and Caroline move into a flat owned by Gertrude Pringle, author of a book on etiquette. Caroline is now Chief Statistician in the Fire Marshall's office of the Ontario government.	**1926** Canadian novelist Margaret Laurence is born in Neepawa, Manitoba, a locale she will feature in much of her fiction. In the U.S., Sinclair Lewis wins the Pulitzer Prize for his novel *Arrowsmith*.

MAZO DE LA ROCHE AND HER TIMES	CANADA AND THE WORLD
	Princess Elizabeth, the future Queen Elizabeth II, is born in London.
1927 Mazo's novel *Jalna* wins the $10,000 *Atlantic Monthly*-Little, Brown competition. The Canadian Authors Association gives her a gala banquet, hosted by Charles G.D. Roberts. *Jalna* reaches third position on the Canadian bestseller list and fifth on the American.	**1927** Sinclair Lewis's *Elmer Gantry* leads both the Canadian and the American bestseller lists.
Mazo begins her next novel, *Whiteoaks of Jalna*.	Poet and animal-story writer Charles G.D. Roberts becomes president of the national Canadian Authors Association, a position he will hold for two years.
1928 The pressure of success leads to another breakdown for Mazo. Caroline resigns her civil service job to become Mazo's nurse, editor, hostess, and secretary.	**1928** Dorothy Livesay publishes *Green Pictures*, her first book of poems, with Macmillan.
	John Galsworthy publishes *Swan Song*, another volume in his popular saga of the Forsyte family.
	British writer Sir Hugh Walpole makes the American fiction bestseller list for the first time with *Wintersmoon*.
1929 Mazo publishes *Whiteoaks of Jalna* to popular and critical acclaim.	**1929** The Great Depression begins with the October stock market crash.
Mazo and Caroline travel to Italy and settle in Devon, England. Mazo meets Canadian actor Raymond Massey and a number of British authors, including Sir Hugh Walpole and Ethel C. Mayne.	British author Ethel C. Mayne publishes her biography of Lady Byron.

Mazo de la Roche

MAZO DE LA ROCHE AND HER TIMES

CANADA AND THE WORLD

1930
Mazo publishes *Portrait of a Dog*, about her beloved Scottish terrier, Bunty.

1931
Mazo's third Jalna novel, *Finch's Fortune*, is published. It reaches number seven on the American bestseller list.

Mazo and Caroline adopt two small children, a girl Esmée and a boy René. The family moves to The Rectory, Hawkchurch, Devon.

1932
Mazo publishes *Lark Ascending* and *The Thunder of New Wings*.

1933
Macmillan releases *The Master of Jalna*. It reaches ninth place on the American bestseller list.

Mazo, Caroline, and the children spend the summer in Canada, at Springfield Farm near Trail Cottage.

1934
While writing another Jalna novel, Mazo also begins working on a play called *Whiteoaks*.

Mazo provides Queen Mary, wife of King George V, with a signed

1930
Sinclair Lewis receives the Nobel Prize in Literature. He is the first American to be so honoured.

1931
Pearl Buck's *The Good Earth* leads the American bestseller list.

Willa Cather's *Shadow on the Rocks*, set in New France, is both a bestseller and a selection of the Book of the Month club.

1932
British novelist John Galsworthy wins the Nobel Prize in Literature.

1933
In the U.S., President Roosevelt implements the New Deal, a program designed to alleviate the effects of unemployment caused by the Great Depression.

In Germany, Adolph Hitler is appointed Chancellor and within a few months becomes a dictator. He suppresses labour unions and harasses Jews.

1934
RKO Radio Pictures of Hollywood releases its movie *Anne of Green Gables* based on the novel by L.M. Montgomery.

MAZO DE LA ROCHE AND HER TIMES	CANADA AND THE WORLD

copy of *Jalna* at the Queen's request.

1935

Mazo, Caroline, and the children are living in England's Malvern Hills.

Young Renny is published.

RKO Hollywood studio releases a movie based on *Jalna*.

1936

Mazo's play, *Whiteoaks*, becomes the first Canadian play to be mounted on a professional London stage.

The sixth Jalna novel, *Whiteoak Harvest*, is published.

1937

Mazo purchases Vale House, near Windsor Castle.

The Very House, Mazo's second book about her children, is published.

1938

Mazo is awarded the Lorne Pierce Medal by the Royal Society of Canada.

1935

Pelham Edgar, Professor of English at the University of Toronto and a friend of Mazo, becomes president of the Canadian Authors Association.

Charles G.D. Roberts becomes Sir Charles when he is knighted by King George V.

1936

The Canadian Broadcasting Corporation (CBC) is created.

The Canadian Authors Association inaugurates the Governor General's Awards for Canadian literature. Initially there are two categories: fiction and non-fiction.

1937

The Canadian Authors Association adds a poetry or drama category to the Governor General's Literary Awards. E.J. Pratt wins the first award for poetry. Laura Salverson wins the fiction category for *The Dark Weaver*, and Stephen Leacock the non-fiction for *My Discovery of the West*.

1938

In Europe, Hitler marches into Austria.

MAZO DE LA ROCHE AND HER TIMES	CANADA AND THE WORLD
Mazo's *Growth of a Man* is published.	In Canada, Emily Carr has her first solo exhibition at the Vancouver Art Gallery.
A Broadway production of *Whiteoaks* opens, with Ethel Barrymore starring.	A nylon bristle toothbrush is now available for purchase. This is the world's first product made of nylon.

1939

Mazo, Caroline, and the children move back to Canada, near Toronto.

1939

The Second World War begins.

Canadian poet and novelist Margaret Atwood is born in Ottawa.

1940

Whiteoak Heritage is published.

1940

Winston Churchill becomes prime minister of Britain.

RKO studio releases the movie *Anne of Windy Poplars*, based on L.M. Montgomery's novel.

1941

Wakefield's Course is published.

1941

Emily Carr wins a Governor General's Literary Award for *Klee Wyck* in the non-fiction category.

1944

Mazo's new novel, *The Building of Jalna*, is published. The British Literary Guild selects it as a book of the month. Mazo receives a cheque for $20,000.

Mazo is the only Canadian author known in Europe. Her Jalna novels represent a free way of life to those oppressed by Hitler and Stalin.

1944

J.F.B. Livesay publishes *Peggy's Cove*, a book that assists this Nova Scotia site in becoming a tourist destination. Dorothy Livesay publishes *Day and Night*, a book of poetry that wins a Governor General's Literary Award.

Ethel Barrymore wins an Academy Award for *None But the Lonely*

MAZO DE LA ROCHE AND HER TIMES	CANADA AND THE WORLD
	Heart, in which she plays opposite Cary Grant.
1945 Mazo's non-fiction book, *Quebec: Historic Seaport*, is published.	**1945** The Second World War ends. The founding conference of the United Nations is held in San Francisco.
	Two Solitudes by Hugh MacLennan wins the Governor General's Literary Award for fiction.
1946 Mazo and Caroline move into a house on Russell Hill Road in Toronto. *Return to Jalna* is published.	**1946** Canadian novelist Frederick Philip Grove publishes a memoir, *In Search of Myself*. Arthur Lower publishes a popular history of Canada, called *Colony to Nation*. Both books win Governor General's Literary Awards.
1947 In September Mazo begins to write again after a gap of a year and a half due to Caroline's being seriously ill.	**1947** Constance Beresford-Howe, a Canadian, is awarded the Dodd-Mead Intercollegiate Literary Fellowship prize for her first novel, *The Unreasoning Heart*, written while she was a student at McGill University. *Bonheur d'Occasion* by French-Canadian writer Gabrielle Roy is published in English as *The Tin Flute* and featured as a selection of the American Literary Guild book club. *The Tin Flute* wins the Governor General's Literary Award for fiction.

Mazo de la Roche

MAZO DE LA ROCHE AND HER TIMES	CANADA AND THE WORLD
	Dorothy Livesay receives the Lorne Pierce Medal and her second Governor General's Literary Award for *Poems for People*.
1948 Mazo is working on the manuscript that will become *Mary Wakefield*. The plot of this new Jalna novel is similar to the plot of *Delight*, written twenty-five years earlier.	**1948** Montreal-based poet A.M. Klein wins a Governor General's Literary Award for *The Rocking Chair and Other Poems*. David Ben-Gurion becomes the first president of the State of Israel.
1949 *Mary Wakefield* is published.	**1949** The Canadian government led by Liberal Prime Minister Louis St. Laurent establishes a Royal Commission on National Development in the Arts, Letters, and Sciences, which becomes known as the Massey Commission after its chair, Vincent Massey.
1951 Mazo wins a National Award medal from the University of Alberta. She publishes *Renny's Daughter*.	**1951** The Massey Commission Report is published. It recommends greater government support for the arts and the creation of an arts funding body in Canada.
1952 Mazo publishes a novella, *A Boy in the House*.	**1952** Elizabeth II becomes Queen of the Commonwealth upon the death of her father, King George VI.
1953 Mazo and Caroline move to their last house at 3 Ava Crescent in Toronto.	**1953** The coronation of Queen Elizabeth II takes place in London.

MAZO DE LA ROCHE AND HER TIMES	CANADA AND THE WORLD
René and Esmée both marry. René's first child is born.	Dwight D. Eisenhower becomes president of the United States.
The Whiteoak Brothers is published.	

1954

Mazo is granted an honorary degree by the University of Toronto.

Variable Winds at Jalna is published. Mazo goes to England to help launch the book.

1957

Mazo's autobiography, *Ringing the Changes*, is published.

Mazo's play, *Whiteoaks*, is broadcast on CBC television.

Mazo is often ill. Rheumatoid arthritis confines her to bed indefinitely, but she keeps on writing.

1954

Children receive the first Salk vaccine to prevent polio.

Ernest Hemingway wins the Nobel Prize in Literature.

1957

The Canada Council is created by an act of Parliament to foster and promote the study and enjoyment of, and the production of works in the arts, humanities, and social sciences. The Canada Council will award financial grants to authors, orchestras, ballet, and drama companies and academics.

Lester B. Pearson wins the Nobel Peace Prize.

John Diefenbaker wins the Canadian federal election and forms a minority Progressive Conservative government.

The U.S.S.R. launches Sputnik 1, the world's first artificial satellite.

1958

Centenary at Jalna is published. This is the fifteenth Jalna book. The saga now spans a century.

1958

Prime Minister Diefenbaker calls a Canadian general election. The Progressive Conservative party

MAZO DE LA ROCHE AND HER TIMES	CANADA AND THE WORLD
Mazo makes her last trip to England.	receives the largest majority ever achieved in the House of Commons.
1959 Mazo turns eighty. She will spend much of her last two years of life in bed due to a variety of illnesses, including Parkinson's Disease. She keeps on writing to the very end.	**1959** The Canadian Authors Association hands over the administration of the Governor General's Literary Awards to the Canada Council.
	The St. Lawrence Seaway, jointly developed by Canada and the U.S., is opened by Queen Elizabeth and President Eisenhower.
1960 *Morning at Jalna* is published.	**1960** American author Harper Lee publishes *To Kill a Mockingbird*.
1961 Mazo de la Roche dies on July 12. She is buried in the graveyard of St. George's Anglican Church beside Lake Simcoe, at Sibbald Point.	**1961** In January, Robert Frost recites his poem "The Gift Out Right" at the inauguration of U.S. President John F. Kennedy.
Delight appears in the prestigious New Canadian Library series, published by McClelland and Stewart.	In April, Yuri Gagarin of the U.S.S.R. is the first man to travel in space. In May, Alan B. Shepard becomes the first American man in space.
1963 The executors of Mazo's estate donate her papers to the University of Toronto.	**1963** U.S. President John F. Kennedy is assassinated in Dallas, Texas.
	1964 Margaret Laurence's *The Stone Angel* is published.

MAZO DE LA ROCHE AND HER TIMES

CANADA AND THE WORLD

The Canadian Parliament, under the guidance of Prime Minister Lester Pearson, reaches agreement on a new Maple Leaf flag for Canada.

1966
Mazo de la Roche of Jalna, a biography by Ronald Hambleton, is published.

1966
Margaret Laurence receives a Canada Council grant.

In China, Mao Zedong launches the People's Cultural Revolution.

1967
The Canadian Centennial is celebrated coast to coast. Montreal hosts millions of visitors at Expo 67 with the theme Man and His World.

The Canada Council initiates an artist-in-residence program.

In the U.S., 50,000 people demonstrate in Washington DC against the Vietnam War.

1968
Caroline Clement turns ninety. She is living alone in the house she shared with Mazo on Ava Crescent in Toronto.

1968
Margaret Atwood receives a Canada Council grant.

Pierre Trudeau becomes leader of the Liberal Party of Canada and wins a general election.

1970
George Hendrick's biography, *Mazo de la Roche*, is published.

1970
Trudeau's government invokes the War Measures Act during the FLQ crisis in Canada.

MAZO DE LA ROCHE AND HER TIMES	CANADA AND THE WORLD
	Margaret Atwood publishes *The Journals of Susanna Moodie*, a book of poetry inspired by Susanna Moodie's life and works.
1972	**1972**
A thirteen-episode CBC television series, *The Whiteoaks of Jalna*, is broadcast.	Canada launches the first communications satellite, Anik, from Cape Canaveral, Florida. Anik will provide for the first satellite transmission of television.
Ronald Hambleton publishes a second biography of Mazo, *The Secret of Jalna*.	Richard Nixon is the first U.S. president to visit Communist China.
Caroline dies on August 3 and is buried next to Mazo.	
	1973
	The Writers Union of Canada is formed "to bring writers together for the advancement of their collective interests."
	1974
	Margaret Laurence's novel *The Diviners* is published and wins the Governor General's Literary Award for fiction.
1984	**1984**
Mazo's adopted son René dies.	Brian Mulroney becomes Prime Minister of Canada.
	1988
	Margaret Atwood's novel *Cat's Eye* is published.
	Canada signs a commercial free trade agreement with the U.S.

MAZO DE LA ROCHE AND HER TIMES	CANADA AND THE WORLD
	1989 In Germany, the Berlin Wall, built in 1961, falls.
1989 Joan Givner publishes *Mazo de la Roche: The Hidden Life*.	**1993** Carol Shields publishes *The Stone Diaries*, which wins Canada's 1993 Governor General's Literary Award for English-language fiction.
1994 *Jalna*, a multimillion-dollar France 2 TV mini-series based on the Whiteoaks saga, is broadcast.	
1995 A museum partly dedicated to Mazo de la Roche is opened: Benares Historic House in Mississauga, Ontario.	**1995** Carol Shields wins the American Pulitzer Prize for fiction for *The Stone Diaries*.
1996 Daniel Bratton publishes *Thirty-Two Short Views of Mazo de la Roche*. A second museum partly dedicated to Mazo de la Roche is opened: Sovereign House in Bronte, Ontario.	

Home of Enos Lundy Senior in Aurora, Ontario today. This home, built by the great-great-grandfather of Mazo de la Roche in 1828, was an important source for the house Jalna. The Lundys also inspired the fictional Whiteoak family in the Jalna novels.

Benares Historic House in Mississauga, Ontario. One of the inspirations for Jalna, Benares is now a museum partly dedicated to Mazo de la Roche.

Sources Consulted

BRATTON, Daniel L. *Thirty-Two Short Views of Mazo de la Roche.* Toronto: ECW Press, 1996.

CLEMENT, Caroline. Interviewed by Ronald Hambleton. Rec. 19 Feb. 1964. Audiotape. University of Toronto. Thomas Fisher Rare Book Library. Mazo de la Roche Ms. Coll. 120, Box 3.

DAVIES, Robertson. *The Well-tempered Critic.* Ed. Judith Skelton Grant. Toronto: McClelland and Stewart, 1981.

DAYMOND, Douglas. "Lark Ascending." *Canadian Literature* 81 (1981): 172-78.

———. "Whiteoak Chronicles: A Reassessment." *Canadian Literature* 66 (1975): 48-62.

DE LA ROCHE, Mazo. Interviewed by Ronald Hambleton. Rec. Jan. 1955. Audiotape. University of Toronto. Thomas Fisher Rare Book Library. Mazo de la Roche Ms. Coll. 120, Box 3.

———. *Beside a Norman Tower.* Toronto: Macmillan, 1934.

———. *Portrait of a Dog.* Toronto: Macmillan, 1930.

———. *Ringing the Changes.* Boston: Little, Brown and Company, 1957.

DUFFY, Dennis. "Mazo de la Roche." *The Oxford Companion to Canadian Literature*. Ed. William Toye. Toronto: Oxford University Press, 1983.

GEORGET, Daniele. "Mazo de la Roche: Un Géant de la Littérature Romanesque." *Paris Match* 7 July 1994: 56-58.

GIVNER, Joan. *Mazo de la Roche: the Hidden Life*. Toronto: Oxford University Press, 1989.

HAMBLETON, Ronald. *Mazo de la Roche of Jalna*. New York: Hawthorn Books, 1966.

———. *The Secret of Jalna*. Toronto: General Publishing, 1972.

HENDRICK, George. *Mazo de la Roche*. New York: Twayne, 1970.

KELL, William [1859-1941]. "Cherry Creek as It Was about 1868." Ms. 1932. Ed. William M. Kell [Barrie, Ont.] 1993.

KIRK, Heather. "Fairytale Elements in the Early Work of Mazo de la Roche." *Wascana Review* 22.1 (1987): 3-17.

———. "Caroline Clement: The Hidden Life of Mazo de la Roche's Collaborator." *Canadian Literature* 184 (2005): 46-67.

———. "The Lundys of Whitchurch as the Whiteoaks of Jalna." *Essays on Canadian Writing*. (2006).

———. "Who Were the Whiteoaks and Where Was Jalna?" Unpublished monograph, 2005.

LIVESAY, Dorothy. "The Making of Jalna: A Reminiscence." *Canadian Literature* 23 (1965): 25- 30.

———. "Mazo Explored." *Canadian Literature* 32 (1967): 57-59.

————. "Foreword: Remembering Mazo." *Selected Stories of Mazo de la Roche*. Ed. Douglas Daymond. Ottawa: University of Ottawa Press, 1979. 11-13.

"Melancholy Accident." *Newmarket Era* 22 Jan. 1886: 2.

PACEY, Desmond. Introduction. *Delight*. By Mazo de la Roche. New Canadian Library 21. Toronto: McClelland and Stewart, 1961. Vii-x.

PANOFSKY, Ruth. "At Odds: Reviewers and Readers of the Jalna Novels." *Studies in Canadian Literature* 25.1 (2000): 57-72.

————. "Don't Let Me Do It: Mazo de la Roche and her Publishers." *International Journal of Canadian Studies* 11 (1995): 171-184.

SYMONS, Scott. "Mazo Was Murdered." Review of *Mazo de la Roche: The Hidden Life*, by Joan Givner. *The Idler* Jan. & Feb. 1990: 53-56.

Sovereign House in Bronte, Ontario.
Now a museum partly dedicated to Mazo de la Roche,
Sovereign House was the setting of *Possession*, her first novel.

Mazo at about age
thirty, on the
Bronte shoreline
beside Lake
Ontario in winter.

Acknowledgments

I thank my husband, Jack Winzer, who helped in too many ways to list here. I also thank the previous biographers of Mazo de la Roche, on whose work I built, especially Ronald Hambleton and Joan Givner. I thank the estate of Mazo de la Roche for allowing me to quote from her work. (All quotations at the beginning of chapters are from Mazo de la Roche's autobiography, *Ringing the Changes*.) I thank Kathy Lowinger of Tundra Books for recommending me for a Writers' Reserve Grant from the Ontario Arts Council. I thank the Ontario Arts Council for its financial support. I thank Rhonda Bailey of XYZ Publishing for her admirable editing. I thank my writer friends for their encouragement.

I also thank the following people – many of them volunteers – who made special efforts to assist me with my research for this book: Bruce Beacock, Archivist, Simcoe County Archives, Midhurst, ON; Clark Bernat and other members of the Niagara Historical Society and Museum, Niagara-on-the-Lake, ON; Susan Blue, Fergus, ON; Tony and Cathy Blue, Aurora, ON; Bill

Bowman, Ontario Genealogical Society, Brantford, ON; Bonnie Bridge, Manitoba Genealogical Society, Winnipeg, MN; Sharon Bunn, Family History Center, Church of Jesus Christ of Latter Day Saints, Barrie, ON; Leah Byzewski, Grand Forks County Historical Society, Grand Forks, ND; Haughton and Jean Clement, Toronto, ON; Keith and Patricia Clement, Thornhill, ON; Anne Corkett, Mono Centre, ON; Jean (Lundy) Daniels, Scarborough, ON.

I thank Bianca de la Roche, Guelph, ON.; Adele Dibben, Hastings County Historical Society, Cannifton, ON; Kenneth and Virginia Douglas, Niagara-on-the-Lake, ON; Bob and Jan Drybrough, Churchill, ON; Ralph and Dorothy Featherstone, Hornby, ON; Marilyn Harry, OGS, Ameliasburg, ON.; Doreen Horton, Barrie, ON; Bert and Elsie Giles, Bronte, ON; Scott Gillies, Museums of Mississauga, Mississauga, ON; Joshua Hanzal, GFCHS, Grand Forks, ND; Anna Hudson, Art Gallery of Ontario, Toronto, ON; Information Services Library Staff of the Aurora Public Library, Barrie Public Library, Belleville Public Library, Brantford Public Library, Mississauga Library System, Newmarket Public Library, and Orillia Public Library; Myrtle Johnson, OGS, North Augusta, ON; Roy Johnson and other members of the Niagara Peninsula Branch, OGS, St. Catherines, ON.

I thank William Kell, Barrie, ON; Linda Kennedy, Research Library, Buffalo and Erie County Historical Society, Buffalo, NY; Olive (Bostwick) Komar, Gormley, ON; Barbara Sayers Larson, Mississauga, ON; John Lennox, York U, Toronto, ON; Gail Lucas, Stroud, ON; Joseph Lundy, Sharon, ON; Barbara Ann

McAlpine and other members of the Bronte Historical Society, Oakville, ON; J. Messmer, Lower Lakes Marine Historical Society, Buffalo, NY; Stephanie Meeuwse, Museums of Mississauga, Mississauga, ON; Ellen Millar and Peter Moran, Archivists, SCA, Midhurst, ON; Roger Nixon, Military and Historical Searches, London, England; Esmée Rees, Toronto, ON; Marion Rhodes, Archivist, Toronto Diocese, Anglican Church of Canada, Toronto, ON; James Rutherford, MGS, Winnipeg, MN; Jean Sarjeant, Orillia Museum, Orillia, ON; Beth Sinyard, Newmarket Museum, Newmarket, ON.

I thank Sandy Slater, Chester Fritz Library, U of North Dakota, Grand Forks, ND; Staff, Thomas Fisher Rare Book Library, U of Toronto, Toronto, ON; Jacqueline Stewart, Aurora Museum, Aurora, ON; Clara Thomas, York U, Toronto, ON; Marjorie Todd, Barrie, ON; Dana Vlasak, Recreation and Parks, City of Mississauga, Mississauga, ON; Ross Wallace, Innisfil Historical Society, Innisfil, ON; Brian Winter, Town of Whitby Archivist, Whitby, ON; Ethel Winzer, Oakville, ON; Jeanne Wright, Holland Landing, ON; Gordon and Nancy Young, Bradford, ON; Jane Zavitz-Bond, Archivist, Canadian Yearly Meeting of the Religious Society of Friends (Quakers), Dorland Room, Pickering College, Newmarket, ON.

Index

Roche, William Richmond (father), 9, 10, 12, 14-19, 24, 25, 29, 31, 32, 35, 36, *48*, 49-51, 55, 56, 59, 61, 63, 64, 66-69, 92, 96, 160-163, 165; birth, 158; death, 69, 70, 76, 166; drifter, 55, 162; marriage, 160
Roche family, 18, 44; conflict with Bryan family, 18
Rogerson, Richard, 44
Rogerson, Mary Catherine, *née* Willson (maternal great-aunt), 8, 23, 43, 44; death, 94
Rogerson family, 44
Roy, Gabrielle, 55, 142, 173
Royal Military College, 47
Royal Society of Canada, 134, 171
Russell Hill Road, Toronto, 137, 173

Scotland, 121
Seckington, 110, 116
Second World War, 129, 136, 142, 172, 173
The Secret of Jalna (biography), 178
Seton, Ernest Thompson, 98
Shakespeare, William, 36
Sharon Temple, 132-134, 158
Shaw, George Bernard, 129, 168
Sibbald Point Provincial Park, 146, 176
Sicily, 119
Simcoe County, 10, 29, 62
Smart Set (magazine), 164
Smith, Walter (cousin), 50
Snow, C.P., 141
Southampton, 121
Sovereign House, 153, 179, *184*
"Spirit of the Dance," 165
Springfield Farm, 170
Stafford Place, London, 128
Star (Toronto), *xii*, 4, 162

Star Weekly (Toronto), 71, 89
St. George's Anglican Church (burial site), 146, *150*, 148, 149, 176
St. Mark's Anglican Church, Toronto, 39
St. Peter's Church, Cherry Creek, 43, *80*, 96
Strawberry Island, 29
Sutton, Ontario, 146
Symons, Scott, 152

Taormina, 109, 114
temperance movement, 57
Tennyson, Alfred Lord, 36
Thomas Fisher Rare Book Library, 147
Thompson brothers' woodware factory. *See* Old Pail Factory, Orillia
Thornhill, Ontario, 137
Through the Looking Glass, 12, 25
The Thunder of New Wings, 83, 84, 155, 167, 170
Times (London), 128
Toronto, 4, 9, 10, 14-16, 18, 19, 22-24, 29, 38, 44, 50, 61, 66, 70, 73, 76, 77, 83, 84, 86, 88, 92, 97, 98, 100, 103, 108, 121, 137, 146, 147, 160-163, 165, 166, 167, 168, 172, 173, 174, 177
Trail Cottage, 84, 89, *90*, 91, 94, 96, 105-107, 121, 137, 168, 170
Traill, Catharine Parr, 152, 159
tuberculosis, 114, 120

United Empire Loyalists, 14, 33
United States, 10, 13, 18, 23, 26, 76, 100, 101, 103, 108, 142, 143, 157, 159, 162, 163, 165, 167, 168, 175-177, 179
University of Alberta, 142, 174

Printed in September 2006
at Marquis,
Cap-Saint-Ignace (Québec).